First World War
and Army of Occupation
War Diary
France, Belgium and Germany

36 DIVISION
109 Infantry Brigade
Royal Inniskilling Fusiliers
1st Battalion
1 February 1918 - 28 March 1919

WO95/2510/1

The Naval & Military Press Ltd
www.nmarchive.com
Published in association with The National Archives

Published by

The Naval & Military Press Ltd

Unit 10 Ridgewood Industrial Park,

Uckfield, East Sussex,

TN22 5QE England

Tel: +44 (0) 1825 749494

www.naval-military-press.com

www.nmarchive.com

This diary has been reprinted in facsimile from the original. Any imperfections are inevitably reproduced and the quality may fall short of modern type and cartographic standards.

© **Crown Copyright**
Images reproduced by permission of The National Archives, London, England, 2015.

Contents

Document type	Place/Title	Date From	Date To
Heading	WO95/2510/1		
Heading	36th Division 109th Infy Bde 1st Bn Roy. Innis. Fus. Feb 1918-Mar 1919 From 29 Div 87 Bde		
Heading	1st Royal Inniskilling Fusiliers. War Diary For Month Of February 1918		
War Diary	Hasler Camp	01/02/1918	06/02/1918
War Diary	Villeselve	07/02/1918	08/02/1918
War Diary	Artemps	09/02/1918	10/02/1918
War Diary	Grd Seraucourt	11/02/1918	15/02/1918
War Diary	St Quentin Front	16/02/1918	22/02/1918
War Diary	Le Hamel	23/02/1918	28/02/1918
Heading	109th Brigade 36th Division. 1st Battalion Royal Inniskilling Fusiliers March 1918 Appendices:- Operation Orders.		
Heading	1st Royal Inniskilling Fusiliers War Diary For Month Of March 1918		
War Diary	Hamel	01/03/1918	05/03/1918
War Diary	Front Line	05/03/1918	06/03/1918
War Diary	Front Line	07/03/1918	09/03/1918
War Diary	Front Line	10/03/1918	18/03/1918
War Diary	Artemps/Hamel	19/03/1918	19/03/1918
War Diary	Hamel	20/03/1918	22/03/1918
War Diary	Flavy-Le-Meldeux	22/03/1918	23/03/1918
War Diary	Flavy-Le-Plessis	24/03/1918	24/03/1918
War Diary	Avricourt	25/03/1918	25/03/1918
War Diary	Varsy	26/03/1918	28/03/1918
War Diary	Wailly	29/03/1918	29/03/1918
War Diary	Famaches	30/03/1918	31/03/1918
Operation(al) Order(s)	1st Battalion The Royal Inniskilling Fusiliers Order No 74	02/03/1918	02/03/1918
Miscellaneous	Administrative Order To Accompany Battalion Order No 74	02/03/1918	02/03/1918
Miscellaneous	Reference Map Grugies Ed. 2A. 66C. N.W. I.		
Operation(al) Order(s)	Great Order No 75	07/03/1918	07/03/1918
Operation(al) Order(s)	Operation Order No 76 By Lt. Col. J.N. Crawford. D.S.O. Commanding 1st Battalion The Royal Inniskilling Fusiliers. In The Field	10/03/1918	10/03/1918
Map			
Heading	109th Brigade. 36th Division. 1st Battalion Royal Inniskilling Fusiliers April 1918		
Heading	1st Royal Inniskilling Fusiliers War Diary For Month Of April 1918 Vol 27		
War Diary	Woincourt	01/04/1918	03/04/1918
War Diary	Dirty Bucket Camp	04/04/1918	05/04/1918
War Diary	Canal Bank	06/04/1918	11/04/1918
War Diary	Front Line Poelcappelle	12/04/1918	16/04/1918
War Diary	Irish Fm Camp C27a5.6	16/04/1918	19/04/1918
War Diary	Front Line	19/04/1918	26/04/1918
War Diary	Irish Fm Camp	26/04/1918	26/04/1918
War Diary	Canal Bank	26/04/1918	30/04/1918

War Diary	Canal Bank	01/04/1918	04/04/1918
War Diary	Front Line	05/04/1918	14/04/1918
War Diary	Canal Bank	14/04/1918	19/04/1918
War Diary	Front Line	19/04/1918	23/04/1918
War Diary	Brielen	23/04/1918	26/04/1918
War Diary	Canal Bank	26/04/1918	30/04/1918
Operation(al) Order(s)	1st Battalion The Royal Inniskilling Fusiliers Order No 78	03/04/1918	03/04/1918
Miscellaneous	Administrative Order To Accompany Battalion Order No 78		
Operation(al) Order(s)	1st Battalion The Royal Inniskilling Fusiliers Order No.79	05/04/1918	05/04/1918
Miscellaneous	Continuation Of Battalion Order No 79	06/04/1918	06/04/1918
Operation(al) Order(s)	1st Battalion The Royal Inniskilling Fusiliers Order No 80	11/04/1918	11/04/1918
Miscellaneous	Administrative Order To Accompany Battalion Order No 80	11/04/1918	11/04/1918
Operation(al) Order(s)	1st Battalion The Royal Inniskilling Fusiliers Order No 81	15/04/1918	15/04/1918
Operation(al) Order(s)	1st-Battalion The Royal Inniskilling Fusiliers Order No 82	19/04/1918	19/04/1918
Operation(al) Order(s)	1st Battalion The Royal Inniskilling Fusiliers Order No 83	25/04/1918	25/04/1918
Operation(al) Order(s)	1st Battalion The Royal Inniskilling Fusiliers Order No 84	26/04/1918	26/04/1918
Miscellaneous	To O.C. "A" Company.		
Diagram etc	St Julien 28 N W Z Parts of Squares C25 1 Scale 1:5000		
Diagram etc	Sheet 28 N W 2 St Julien Parts Of Squares C 17 18 22 23 24 28 29		
Heading	1st Royal Inniskilling Fusiliers War Diary For Month Of May 1918 Vol 28		
War Diary	Canal Bank	30/05/1918	31/05/1918
Heading	War Diary Of 1st Battalion The Royal Inniskilling Fus From 1st June 1918 To 30th June 1918		
War Diary	Front Line	01/06/1918	02/06/1918
War Diary	Utline	03/06/1918	04/06/1918
War Diary	Tonnellers Camp	05/06/1918	08/06/1918
War Diary	Cassel & Rubrouck Areas	08/06/1918	16/06/1918
War Diary	Tunnellers Camp	17/06/1918	20/06/1918
War Diary	Pekin Camp	21/06/1918	30/06/1918
Heading	War Diary Of 1st Battalion The Royal Inniskilling Fusiliers From 1st July 1918 To 31st July 1918		
War Diary	Rossendaal Area	01/07/1918	14/07/1918
War Diary	Mt De Cats	14/07/1918	24/07/1918
War Diary	Mt Noir	24/07/1918	01/08/1918
Heading	War Diary Of 1st Battalion Royal Inniskilling Fusiliers From 1st August 1918 To 31st August 1918 Vol 31		
War Diary	Front Line Left Subsector St Jans Cappel	01/08/1918	05/08/1918
War Diary	Mt Noir	05/08/1918	08/08/1918
War Diary	Mont Des Cats	08/08/1918	24/08/1918
War Diary	Front Line	24/08/1918	31/08/1918
Heading	War Diary Of 1st Royal Inniskilling Fusiliers From 1st Sept 1918 To 30th Sept 1918		
War Diary		01/09/1918	29/09/1918

Heading	War Diary Of 1st Battalion The Royal Inniskilling Fusiliers From 1st October 1918 To 31st October 1918 Vol 33		
War Diary		01/10/1918	31/10/1918
War Diary	St Annes	01/11/1918	14/11/1918
War Diary	Roncq	15/11/1918	30/11/1918
War Diary	Roncq	03/12/1918	28/02/1919
War Diary		24/02/1919	24/02/1919
Miscellaneous	The D A G Office 3rd Echelon		
War Diary	Roncq	01/03/1919	02/03/1919
War Diary	Mouseron	03/03/1919	17/03/1919
War Diary	Dunkerque	18/03/1919	28/03/1919

36TH DIVISION
109TH INFY BDE

1ST BN ROY. INNIS. FUS.

FEB 1918-MAR 1919

FROM ~~29 DIV~~
~~96~~
87 Bde

1st Royal Inniskilling Fusiliers.

W A R   D I A R Y

for

MONTH OF FEBRUARY, 1918.

WAR DIARY
or
INTELLIGENCE SUMMARY

(Erase heading not required.)

Volume 35

Army Form C. 2118.

Hour, Date, Place		Summary of Events and Information	Remarks and references to Appendices
HASLER CAMP	Feb 1/4	Working parties employing 150 men under R.E. supervision working on tramways. Training of Specialists. 2nd Lt. O'Brien D.S.O. returns from leave & proceeds on Musketry Course. 2nd Lt. McClelland on Bombing Course.	
"	5/6	The Battn. moves to the 36th Division being transferred from the 29th Div. Entrains at Wamerlinghe and detrains at HAM marching to VILLESELVE. Lt. Baker admitted to Hospital.	Vide Bn Order No 68
VILLESELVE	7	Re-organisation of the Battn. 130 O.R. joined Bn from Re-inforcement Camp. from the 10th Bn taken on strength. 7 officers & 150 O.R. joined for duty. Lt. Q.M. DeLacey M.C.	
"	8	The Battn. moves to ~~Battn~~ ARTEMPS & comes under orders of the G.O.C. 109 Infy. Bde.	Vide Bn Order No 69
ARTEMPS	9	Battn provides working parties employing whole Battn under R.E. supervision. Effective Str. 42 offs. 1069 O.R. Battn proceeds to Gd. SEREAUCOURT	
"	10	The Battn proceeds to Gd. SEREAUCOURT. Working Battn str. 26 offs 1938 O.R. Working parties employing about 600 men return for Battle zone proceeding in advance. The Battn is now in Brigade Reserve. The Battn inspected by G.O.C. Division	Vide Bn Order No 70
Gd Sereaucourt	11/14	Working parties employing 600 men working under R.E. supervision in Battle zone. 2/Lt Balkan rejoined from Hospital	

WAR DIARY
or
INTELLIGENCE SUMMARY

Army Form C. 2118.

Volume 35

Hour, Date, Place	Summary of Events and Information	Remarks and references to Appendices
GRD SEREAUCOURT 14	2nd Lt Roland proceeded to Sanctuary Course and 2nd Lt W. Morrison rejoined from leave.	
" 15	The Battn proceeds to take over the left sub-sector of the line before ST QUENTIN from the 2nd R.I.R. Advance party leaves at 9 A.M. & takes over communication. The remainder of the Battn. leave at 6.45 P.M. The last relief being completed about 11 P.M. the Battn H.Q. established at (Ref Sheet 66c NW Edition 2) A 3 D 8.2. and Right (A) Co. H.Q at A 5 B 1.9. Left Co. (B) H.Q at (Ref Sheet 62 BSW Edition 3.3) S 28 B 3.4 and Support Co. H.Q at S 28 A 8.3. D Coy H.Q. (reserve assistance Coy) isolated by the side of Bn H.Q. S 28 D 9.6 where the Railway crosses Road to the Canal Bank. 2nd Lt McLean proceeded to 18th Corps Instruction Course and 2nd Lt Lawrence to Bde Riding School.	Vide Battn Order No 71 See map attached to orders.
ST. QUENTIN FRONT 16	Enemy shelled the vicinity of "A" (right) Coy. H.Q intermittently from 6.30 A.M. to 10.30 A.M. Occasionally sniping from enemy about the Graveyard through which front of the Right Company runs. Practically all our trenches both forward & reserve are under observation from the enemy lines and ST QUENTIN. One patrol from A Coy. one from B were sent out during night to investigate trouble in front of their trenches — they were formed up and found 25 O.R.'s. R.Rh Sta. 884 O.R. Effec St2 4 Ofrs 1003 O.R.	
" 17/19	Very little enemy activity — especially artillery.	

WAR DIARY
or
INTELLIGENCE SUMMARY

Army Form C. 2118.

Volume 35

Hour, Date, Place	Summary of Events and Information	Remarks and references to Appendices
ST QUENTIN FRONT 19/19 Feb	Enemy Snipers fairly active by day & machine guns by night. Considerable work done in improving our trenches. Patrols sent out each night by A Coy & B Coy examining enemy wire - few gaps were found. On the night of the 19th Companies relieved each other i.e. A Coy relieved B and D Coy relieved A. Relief completed by 10.15 P.M.	
" 20/21	Very quiet in this Sector. Occasional Sniping and machine gun fire at night. Working parties employed on Trenches & strong points. Considerable air activity - both our own & Enemy's. Patrols out each night reconnoitring enemy wire - which has been found in good order. No gaps.	Vide Bn Order No 72
" 22	The Battn is relieved by the 18th (Lancashire Hussars) Bn The King's (Liverpool) Reg.T of the 30th Div. who are Taking over this portion of the Divisional Front. Relief completed by 10.15 P.M. The Battn proceeds such to LE HAMEL & becomes the Battn in Reserve.	Vide Battn order No 73
LE HAMEL 23	Working Parties employing about 200 men under R.E's in the Battle zone. General cleaning up & baths. Ration Str 26 ops 689 O.R. Effec. Str. 41 ops 1086 O.R.	

Army Form C. 2118.

WAR DIARY
or
INTELLIGENCE SUMMARY

(Erase heading not required.)

Volume 36

Hour, Date, Place		Summary of Events and Information	Remarks and references to Appendices
LE HAMEL	24	Working Parties employing the whole Battn working on the Battle Zone under R.E. Supervision. Training of Specialists. 2nd Lt R. McConnell returned from leave.	
"	25/26	Working Parties employing whole Battn under R.E's Supervision on the Battle Zone. Capt Moore proceeded on leave & 2nd Lt Stephenson appointed A/Adjt during his absence. 2nd Lts McConnell, S. Robinson, & McLelland reported from Bovves.	
"	27.	Test at 8.15AM to man the Battle Zone, which is situated about two miles N. of LE HAMEL. The Companies & Hdqrs had taken up their positions by 8.40AM. Working Parties employed after on work in the Battle Zone. Training of Specialists.	
"	28.	The Battn provides working Parties for work under R.E Supervision on Battle Zone. Training of Specialists. Orders received at mid-day to stand by in readiness to man Battle zone. Lt Bell & 2nd Lt O'Brien D.S.O reported Battn from leave.	B/f.

1247 W 3299 200,000 (E) 8/14 J.B.C. & A. Forms/C. 2118/11.

109th Brigade.
36th Division.

1st BATTALION

ROYAL INNISKILLING FUSILIERS

MARCH 1918

Appendices :-
Operation Orders.

WA 26

109/36

1ST ROYAL INNISKILLING FUSIRS.

WAR DIARY

FOR

MONTH OF MARCH 1918.

WAR DIARY or **INTELLIGENCE SUMMARY**
Army Form C. 2118.

(Erase heading not required.)

Volume 16 — 1st R. Innis. Killing Fus.

Hour, Date, Place	Summary of Events and Information	Remarks and references to Appendices
March		
1/2	Now on Island the enemy occupying positions from the ridge to almost 200 yds South of them (taken by 2 Offs 705.OR yesterday). 11.0pp 105OR left base reinforce troops.	
3	I wired to 2i/Div O sent one Coy and O. NF yesterday to help complete 40 ts.Or wounded as 17 to 16 to file artillery fire being active on both sides.	
4	A mixed company of about 80 Boers was observed approaching our lines at about 11.30 am. It was shortly engaged with Lewis gun machine rifle fire etc. commanded by Col D pady under Colonel Van Rensburg who have taken over command. Open ground to fast line. As a result the enemy was dispersed leaving two wounded and ten unwounded prisoners in our hands. Others of the enemy were observed to fly but escaped. Another party which was customary the Boers we opened our fight. Company was 15 minutes firing and got back with thirteen of Bowers party 16 105R Innis Rifles left our line at 11.30pm. They will get camped of Naabe pokadrp Boadowne on Sunday 13th.	Was Bn Order Attached
5	Mn Artillery Service was active. Duties only the in Section very quiet on every way. A few enemy planes	

WAR DIARY or INTELLIGENCE SUMMARY

Army Form C. 2118.

Hour, Date, Place	Summary of Events and Information	Remarks and references to Appendices
Mar. 5	[illegible] patrol of our line at the [illegible] by a [illegible] at B7a [illegible] and patrolled [illegible] and the enemy wire. No enemy were sighted. Enemy artillery active, [illegible] somewhat scattered. Our artillery [illegible]. The patrol reported in at 11.0 p.m. The enemy encountered.	
6		
7 B.C.B.V./Nab.7	Our artillery registering again. The enemy's howitzer guns [illegible] field [illegible] active. Our [illegible] [illegible] very more cautious [illegible] when [illegible] our wire line relieved by the two companies in support. A patrol of [illegible] [illegible] left at B.1.K.0.28 and [illegible] both an a S.W. to B. [illegible]. [illegible] the enemy's trenches.	See Pru. a. 7/3/15 attached
8	[illegible] [illegible]. I received orders at 4 April [illegible] the line at B.1.6.3.1 to reconnoitre enemy wire in 30a. A strong battle party was stationed at B.1.d.1. The patrol returned.	
9	Our artillery very active. No reply from enemy side. Quiet. A patrol went up from our railway cutting at B.7.a.2.7.6 [illegible] to long [illegible] working parties which might be working on the new [illegible] forward during the day at B.1.d.1. The patrol [illegible] the [illegible] out. No enemy party was encountered.	

Army Form C. 2118.

WAR DIARY
or
INTELLIGENCE SUMMARY
(Erase heading not required.)

Volume 36

Hour, Date, Place	Summary of Events and Information	Remarks and references to Appendices
Front Line 10	Front Line Quiet. A patrol expected to fall into hostile working party bivouacking at head was fired on. Reply was heavy. Fire kept up for an appreciable and retired them on our part. Few men opened with Lewis Machine Gun on their patrol. It is not known what casualties to our own.	
" 11	Quiet as regards. The BN is relieved by the 9th Bn R Inniskn. The relief was complete by 10.15pm BN proceeded to ARTEMPS. During the whole of the last four companies has found working parties to work on the Keep—forming firestepping and deepening trenches, adopting them, and in the event of a trench attack to act as local and heavy garrisons.	
12th	Training	
" 13	St Patricks Day and a holiday. Inter Battalion Sports with the 2nd Bn R Inn Fus	
" 18	Training	

WAR DIARY
or
INTELLIGENCE SUMMARY

Army Form C. 2118.

Hour, Date, Place	Summary of Events and Information	Remarks and references to Appendices
Winterville 19	Took on the Battle Zone. The French started	See Pl. A. 2091.
Hamel 20th	Work on Battle Zone.	
21st	At 5 am the order is received to man the Battle Zone. 66 CME. The Battalion got into position	
6 pm	The enemy shelled heavily during the day with HE and gas shells, especially on B Coy front. About 8 pm enemy were seen advancing on our position in artillery formation but did not carry out an attack. This day, hostile artillery slackened about 6 pm.	
22nd	About 6 am the enemy started shelling our lines again. About 11 am enemy they started to concentrate in dead ground about 1000 x in front of our line and in the village of FONTAINE	

WAR DIARY
or
INTELLIGENCE SUMMARY

(Erase heading not required.)

Army Form C. 2118.

Hour, Date, Place	Summary of Events and Information	Remarks and references to Appendices
	At 1pm he strongly attacked B Coy and was driven back with heavy casualties. About 1.30 he heavily attacked the right of B Coy and succeeded in penetrating into our lines in the centre. Both A and B Coys. Counter-attacked to the counter attack (company C Coy). Orders were received for B Coy to be held on long as possible. The enemy heavily attacked this line and hundreds of it heavy casualties being inflicted on him. At about 2.30pm an order was received to retire into the battalion redoubt held by D Coy. The enemy continued to attack and succeeded in almost surrounding the redoubt. There was heavy fighting round the redoubt. About 40 men succeeded in cutting their way through the enemy and retired.	

WAR DIARY
or
INTELLIGENCE SUMMARY

(Erase heading not required.)

Army Form C. 2118.

Hour, Date, Place	Summary of Events and Information	Remarks and references to Appendices

The Battalion suffered the following casualties in this action:-

Officers. Killed. 2Lieut JP Robinson. 2Lieut AJS Dick.
2Lieut H.M.Hamilton. 2Lieut G.O'Brien DSO. Lieut S M^cD.Aitchison.

Wounded. Capt L R Woorley MC.
Lieut Col J N Crawford DSO. Capt
Capt T H Cochburn Mercer. Capt E E J Moore. Lieut B L Griggs
Capt J McMeehan. 2Lieut W Price MC. 2Lieut C.Gregg
Lieut W.C. Baker. 2Lieut S McConnell. 2Lieut S.S Hunter.
Capt G W Wilcock. Lieut F S Marchant. 2Lieut R B McConnell
Capt Hodgson Jones. (RAMC attached)
Wounded and Missing. 2Lieut E R Palmer.

Men. Missing 531.

WAR DIARY or INTELLIGENCE SUMMARY

Army Form C. 2118.

Place	Date	Hour	Summary of Events and Information	Remarks and references to Appendices
FLAVY-LE-MELDEUX	23rd		The transport lay at FLAVY.	
	23rd	11pm	Orders were received to fall out all details of Band, QM stores etc; there were added to the CR who had marched from front line at HAMEL making in all 100 OR. with no officers except CSM Hardy. These were put under command of Major RS Knox DSO with details of the Battalion & other 109th Brigade. Under orders received they were organised into 4 platoons under 4 junior officers of the 9th R Innis Fus and sent forward to form a defensive flank to 30th Division who had retired on ESMERY-HALLON. (A line was taken up from BONNEUIL CHATEAU through P29 c.90.00 – P29 a.20.70 for the afternoon & details on our right, then dug in on the line. No attack was made by enemy. Men dug in on approximately same	
			At 10 pm by verbal order of Brigadier Major 109 Brigade all details were ordered to march on GOULENCOURT to rendezvous 9th R Innis Fus and report at FLAVY crossroads for orders. At midnight verbal orders were received by OC arrival of the advance guard platoon at GOULENCOURT and was fired on AMBUSH by the enemy, rapid fire being opened up by infantry and a M.G. in village and cross-roads – fire was covered by being carried flanks of village. A total casualties caused. The force withdrew to crossroads FLAVY-LE-PLESSIS and orders issued for from Brigade. On receipt of orders at 5.30 am. 24th.	
FLAVY-LE-PLESSIS	24th	5.30am	A position was taken up W. of LE-PLESSIS, covering entrance where in touch with 4th French Regt. Men dug in again. During the afternoon the French on Right Sector of GOULENCOURT being heavily attacked and at 16 pm commenced to retire. Under orders of Major Knox, we fell back to form a flank at crossroads FLAVY-LE-PLESSIS where they rendezvous'd	

WAR DIARY or INTELLIGENCE SUMMARY

Army Form C. 2118.

Place	Date	Hour	Summary of Events and Information	Remarks and references to Appendices
AVRICOURT	25th		until ordered at 11 p.m. to retire through the French 2nd Line to reform transport at FRETOY.	
VARSY	26th	9 am	The attack & transport marched via BLAGNY to AVRICOURT where the Battalion was reorganised into 4 companies. Capt. Hamilton in Command. Total strength exclusive of transport 8 officers 147 O.R. At 6-20 p.m. orders were received to take up a new billet for VARSY where Batts. was billeted for the night. 64 9 am. Batts. stood to and was ordered to take up a position in support of 9th R. INNIS. FUS. Extending their right flank from Q.19.a.90.90 to new AVRE with orders to get in touch with French South of river. During the day we received information that the advanced posts of 9th R. INNIS. FUS. on left and French on right had been driven in & village was in enemy hands. During the night advanced posts were two helped our their bank to cover off craft. Heavy fighting & rifle fire occurred on left and one attack was launched on 9th INNIS. FUS. front particularly retired on our lines. We were reorganised & reoccupied their line.	
	27th	5 am	Orders were received to retire on 2nd Line in Q.24. This line two from left 9th R. Innis. Fus. Completed steadily and we withdrew in good order by platoons leaving covering parties. At 7.30 am information was received that the R. INNIS. FUS. on left had not been able to get away so we were ordered forward to organise positions to gain Cozy. right this was done. About 9 am heavy fighting developed own front. A large volume of enemy could be seen advancing against French own front. Enemy advance and line moved in and evening to the German advance on the left. We were ordered to resume position in Q.23.	

Army Form C. 2118.

WAR DIARY
or
INTELLIGENCE SUMMARY.
(Erase heading not required.)

Place	Date	Hour	Summary of Events and Information	Remarks and references to Appendices
	28th	7 a.m.	Fire was opened by platoons covered by 2nd R. Innis. Fus., but owing to further change in situation all were ordered to retire across road and join french who were retiring east along the line. The withdrawal was covered and an good order, across the river we came under machine gun fire. full Coys in small groups on GUERBIGNY–MONTDIDIER road where we reformed & under the Brigadier orders marched near RATIBUS & BOUILLANCOURT where we billeted for the night.	
			We marched to CHIRMONT when command was taken by Major Pont M.C. About 1 p.m. news received that the enemy has taken MONTDIDIER & the Brigade receive orders to march to COULLEMELLE with all rapidity, precautions to be south side up a position covering our artillery W. of village. The battalion took up a position from T.15.c.3.8. — T.15.d.2.9. K.B.C. Coys being in the front line & D in reserve, on the village, with the 2nd and 2nd Batts on the left, no action followed. The transport marched to CHAPISSY EPAGNY. The Batts to relieved by the 9th Batts & go into billets in COULLEMELLE. About 2 p.m. the situation is normal & the Brigade marches to EPAGNY & go in to billets ab. 20.45. the Brigade marches to WAILLY via JUMEL & go into billets accompanied by transport.	
WAILLY	29th		The Brigade leaves WAILLY at 15.30 & marches to SALEUX to entrain for CAMACHES area. Transport marched by road staging at ALLERY.	
CAMACHES.	30th		The Brigade entrains at 1.11 am & detrains at EU about 16.30. The latter marches to NOINCOURT & go into billets.	
	31st			

A Bowen Major
R. Smith Killing Major

SECRET   Copy No. " ".

1ST BATTALION THE ROYAL INNISKILLING FUSILIERS ORDER NO. 74.

2nd. March 1918.

Reference Maps:-
            66C N.W.I. 1/10,000.
            Edition I.A.

1.   The Battalion will relieve 2nd. Bn. Royal Inniskilling
    Fusiliers on the night 3/4th. March 1918.

2.   "A" Company will relieve "C" Co. 2nd. R. Innis. Fus.
        "B"   "   "   "   "D" "   "   "   "   "
        "C"   "   "   "   "B" "   "   "   "   "
        "D"   "   "   "   "A" "   "   "   "   "
    One guide for each Platoon and one Guide per Coy. Hd. Qrs., will
    be at Cross Roads by Bn. Hd. Qrs., at 6.30. p.m.

3.   Bn. Hd. Qrs., will be established at A.17.d.2.4 at 6.45. p.m.

4.   Companies will parade in their Company Lines and will
    march off as under.
        Hd. Qr. Coy., will move off at 5.15. p.m.
        D "X" Company   "   "   " " 5.20. p.m.
        A " "   "   "   "   " " 5.27. p.m.
        B " "   "   "   "   " " 5.34. p.m.
        C " "   "   "   "   " " 5.41. p.m.
    100 yards interval between Platoons will be observed.

5.   Dress:- Marching Order, Steel Helmets. Box respirators
                    at the ALERT.

6.   Route:- GRAND SERACOURT   X Roads A.17.d.

7.   Completion of relief will be reported to Bn. Hd. Qrs.

8.   All defence schemes, aeroplane photographs will be taken
    over.

9.   ACKNOWLEDGE.

                        R.W. Stephenson   2/Lieut. & A/Adjt.
                    1st. Bn. The Royal Inniskilling Fusiliers.

Copies to
    1 & 2. Staff.
    3 & 4. War Diary.
    5. 2nd. Bn. Royal Innis. Fus.
    6, 7, 8 & 9. Companies.
    10. Qr. Mr.
    11. T.O.
    12. M.O.

SECRET.

ADMINISTRATIVE ORDER TO ACCOMPANY BATTALION ORDER NO.74.

2nd. March 1918.

1. BLANKETS.
All Blankets and surplus stores will be stacked at the Guard Room, labelled and rolled in bundles of 10, by 10.a.m. to-morrow.

2. TRANSPORT.
(a) The Transport Officer will arrange for 2 limbers to report to each Company Headquarters at 4.0.p.m. to-morrow.
Lewis Guns, rations, rations, dixies, Officers Kits and Mess boxes will be loaded on these limbers.
The limbers will proceed with the Companies.

(b) The German Wagon and Maltese Cart will report to Bn. Hd.Qrs., at 4.0.p.m. to-morrow and proceed in rear of Headquarters.

3. TRENCH STORES.
O.C. Companies will render to Orderly Room by 10.a.m. 4th. inst., a list of all trench stores taken over.

4. SYNCHRONIZATION OF WATCHES.
An Orderly will report to Company Commanders before 12 noon in order to sychronize watches.

L.W.Shpaderson 2/Lieut. & A/Adjt.
1st. Bn. The Royal Inniskilling Fusiliers.

Copies to:-
All recipients of Bn. Order No. 74.

SECRET INSTRUCTIONS.   Copy No. "3".

Reference Map GRUGIES Ed.2A.66C.N.W.I.

1. A Raid will be carried out on the night 4/5th, by the 15th, Royal Irish Rifles from our trenches.

2. <u>Object of the Raid</u>. To obtain an identification and to kill Germans. A prisoner alive or dead must be brought in.

3. The post to be raided will be one at B7.b.25.45.

4. The Raiding party will consist of 4 Officers and 36th.Other Ranks, divided into four parties. Point of departure from our trenches will be at B7.b.25.35.
    The Leading party (closely followed by the remaining three parties) will lay a tape to the point of entering enemy's trenches which will be at B.7.b.58.52.
    After the raid all parties will return along the tape to the point of departure from our trenches.

5. <u>Dress</u>:- Parties will be dressed as follows:-
            Box respirators will not be carried.
   Head dress:- Cap comforter or cap with badge removed.
            Faces and hands will be blackened

6. O.C. Companies will take steps to inform all ranks of above and to warn them not to discuss operations before they take place.
    They will also do all in their power to assist the raiding party.

7. Zero hour will be notified later.

8. <u>ACKNOWLEDGE</u>.

9. No patrols will be sent out during the raid.

                        (Sd) R.W.W. Stephenson. 2/Lieut & A/Adjutant.
                                      Great.

Copies to
    1. Staff.
    2 & 3. War Diary.
    5 6 & 7. Companies
    8. O.C. Raiding Party.
    9. File.

SECRET.   Copy No. "3".

GREAT ORDER No. 75.

7th. March 1918.

1. The Two Companies in the Front Line will be relieved to-night.

2. "C" Company will relieve "B" Company.
   Relief will not commence before 6.0.p.m.

   "D" Company will relieve "A" Company.
   Relief will not commence before 9.0.p.m.

3. Details of Relief will be arranged mutually between Company Commanders concerned.

4. Watson Fans and Ground Flares will NOT be handed over, if Companies have any surplus after completion the Officers and N.C.O's, the surplus will be handed over to the Adjutant.

5. Ration Limbers will collect mess stores, kits etc., and convey them to New Headquarters.

6. Completion of Relief will be reported to Battalion Headquarters by the surname of the Company Commander.

7. ACKNOWLEDGE.

                                        R W Stephenson
                                        2/Lieut.& A/Adjutant.
                GREAT.

Copies to
    1 & 2. Staff.
    3 & 4. War Diary.
    5 6 7 & 8. Companies.
    9. Qr.Mr.

S E C R E T. OPERATION ORDER No. 76. Copy No 4
BY
LT. COL. J. N. CRAWFORD. D.S.O.
COMMANDING 1ST BATTALION THE ROYAL INNISKILLING FUSILIERS.
IN THE FIELD.   10th. MARCH 1918.

1. (a) The 9th. Bn. Royal Inniskilling Fusiliers will relieve the 1st. Bn. The Royal Inniskilling Fusiliers on the night 11/12th. March 1918.

   (b) On relief the Battalion will march to ARTEMPS and take over billets vacated by the 2nd. Battalion Royal Inniskilling Fusiliers, and be the Training Battalion.

2. All Trench Stores, Photographs, Watson Fans etc., will be handed over to the relieving Unit and copy of receipt sent to Battalion Headquarters not later than 9.0.a.m. on the 12th. inst.
   In addition each Company will hand over a map showing dispositions and strength of Posts and Keeps, also a list of KEEP stores.

3. Guides One guide per Platoon and one guide per Company Headquarters will be at cross roads by Battalion Headquarters by 6.30.p.m.

4. Order of Relief will be notified later.

5. Completion of Relief will be reported to Battalion Headquarters by the surname of the Company Commander.

6. ACKNOWLEDGE.

                                        RW Stephenson 2/Lieut. & A/Adjt.
                                        1st. Bn. The Royal Inniskilling Fusiliers.

Copies to
    1 & 2. Staff.
    3 & 4. War Diary.
    5.6.7.& 8. Companies.
    9. 9th. Bn. Royal Innis. Fus.
    10. Qr. Mr.
    11. M.O.
    12. M.O.

Scale 1/500

19
24
26
30
A
F

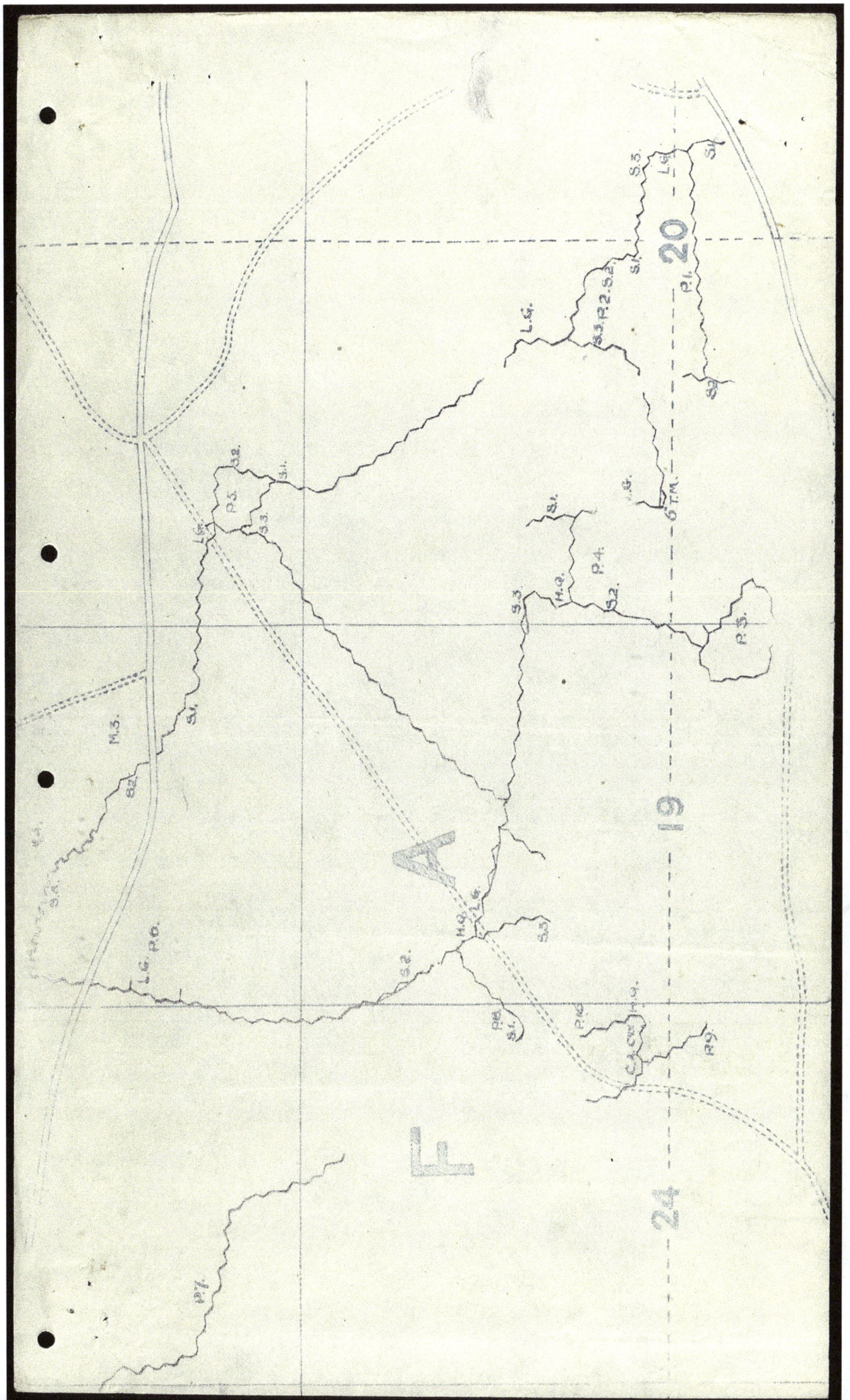

109th Brigade.
36th Division.

1st BATTALION

ROYAL INNISKILLING FUSILIERS

APRIL 1918.

Battalion Orders attached.
Account of Operations attached to Brigade H.Q. Diary.

1ST ROYAL INNISKILLING FUSILIERS.

WAR DIARY

for MONTH OF APRIL, 1918.

WAR DIARY
or
INTELLIGENCE SUMMARY

Army Form C. 2118.

(Erase heading not required.)

Volume 37

Hour, Date, Place	Summary of Events and Information	Remarks and references to Appendices
WOINCOURT April 1	The Battalion rests and reorganises.	
2	Reorganisation continued. 11 officers 93 OR from the 23rd Northumberland Battalion report and are taken on the strength.	
3	Reorganisation continued. The Battalion accompanied by first Van transport entrains at WOINCOURT for ROUSBRUGGE at 2200 hours. See Bn Order 78	
DIRTY BUCKET CAMP 4	The Battalion detrains at ROUSBRUGGE 11.30 am and proceeds in busses to HOSPITAL FARM Bivd 21 Under the Battalion Orders No 18.	
5	Reorganisation. The Army Commander Addresses the officers of the 109th Bde in Church Army hut. At 2.15pm Bn Order no 19	
CANAL BANK 6	The Battalion proceeds to Support Area CANAL BANK March H 13.20 hours. 'C'coy on the right 109 Inf Bde Order No 18 Bank. A and B companies in Bn H.Q. Zone Coode-Cnidrancelport in Sing and Reform Scheme	
	Comp Draft of 300 OR anks reports at 19.30	
7th	On April A Company transp in to those relieved KEMPTON PARK C.15.B.3.5 Reorganisation and training. Draft of 50 OR and arrives on the 9th	
11th	A Coy heav composed of the Enniskillen officers and officers and Signallers from each company and 1 NCO from each platoon go forward to take over from 2nd Royal Irish Rifles and the first from	
	trench strength off is 16 OR Say Rifle strength off 13. OR 734	

WAR DIARY
or
INTELLIGENCE SUMMARY

Army Form C. 2118.

Place	Date	Hour	Summary of Events and Information	Remarks and references to Appendices
FRONT LINE POELCAPPELLE	12th	7.30 pm	The Battalion proceeded to take over the front line from 2/ Royal Irish Rifles. C & D Coys and HQrs marched off at 7.30 pm and entrained at EXETER C.25.b.5.8. at 8.15 pm. A & B Coys proceeded by march route. Dispositions as follows: C & D in front line. D Co. 1 platoon V.21.c.1.5. 1 platoon V.21.c.0.2. 1 platoon and Co HQrs V.20.c.8.8. C Co. 1 platoon V.20.b.2.8. 1 platoon V.14.b.2.4. 1 platoon V.14.c.9.4. 1 platoon & Co HQrs V.20.a.9.9. A Co. POELCAPPELLE defences & HQrs V.19.b.6.4. B Co. Reserve DELTA HOUSE V.19.C.3.2. Battalion HQrs NORFOLK HOUSE V.19.a.6.1. Relief reported complete at 11.30 pm.	Vide B.O. No 80.
	13th		Enemy artillery very quiet. Occasional short bursts of machine gun fire during the night.	
	13/14		A patrol of 1 Officer & 3 ORs left our lines at TRACAS FARM at 2.15 am returning at 3.15 am; no hostile posts were encountered. Another patrol left SPRIET at 2 am. Is reconnoitred pill boxes at OXTON & NOBLES FM.	
	14th		At 2.15 am an enemy patrol of 6 men approached our post at NOBLES Fm. V.14.d.2.3. The garrison of the post fired on them and cries were heard. It was discovered at day light that 1 man was killed. It is believed that another was wounded. The NCO in charge of the platoon Sgt ROE and L/Cpl ROBERTSON showed great initiative and by quickly grasping the situation, inflicted casualties on the enemy and obtained a valuable identification. Machine gun fire directed on our front line & trench during the night.	

Army Form C. 2118.

WAR DIARY
or
INTELLIGENCE SUMMARY.
(Erase heading not required.)

Instructions regarding War Diaries and Intelligence Summaries are contained in F. S. Regs., Part II. and the Staff Manual respectively. Title pages will be prepared in manuscript.

Place	Date	Hour	Summary of Events and Information	Remarks and references to Appendices
	14/15		Enemy artillery fairly quiet, slight T.M. activity against left front of front line. A patrol went out from V14 C.9.4. and found pill box at V14 d.0.7. unoccupied. Sounds of taps and work were observed from huts in front of NOBLES FARM identified 103rd R.I.R. About 6.5 am two of the enemy approached NOBLES FM; the garrison tried (5 came in bus) they were driven off were fired on & dear.	
	15/16		Enemy artillery fairly quiet. Machine gun action at night. No one Very lights than usual were fired by enemy during the night. The Bn was withdrawn from the front line again in accordance with Battalion Orders 81	Bn Order 81

WAR DIARY or INTELLIGENCE SUMMARY

Army Form C. 2118.

Place	Date	Hour	Summary of Events and Information	Remarks and references to Appendices
IRISH FM. CAMP C.27a.5.6.	16th		Battalion comes into camp at IRISH FM C.27a.5.6. All companies reported in camp by 1pm. The Battalion becomes Support Battalion to the 9th Bn in front line system and is under orders to man battle zone at half an hours notice. All companies accommodated in camp. Dispositions in Battle Zone:— A.Coy. 2 Platoons C.28 a 30.30 to C.28 a 10.85 1 Platoon Bn Hqrs ENGLISH FM C.27 B 50.20. B.Coy. 2 Platoons C.22 d 90.60 to C.22 c 30.00 1 Platoon Bn Hqrs HOLT C.27 c 90.85 C.Coy in trenches C.27 a 50.45. Bn HQ C.27 a 45.85 Alternative artillery subject to carrying shelters & Camels during the night a few shell movements. About Bny parade at 5AM for wire under RE putting up wire. Comd B.Coy sent work at	Sheet 28 NW2.
	17th		9AM on shelter in trench in front of the camp C.27 a 50.45 to C.27 a 45.90 in case of bombardment of the camp. The Battn in the camp are put to work and material left behind by former occupants collected.	
			Day is moved into Artillery shelters C.21.c.5.2. Practice Alarm Battle Zone at 5pm.	
	18th		2 Platoons of A.Coy 2 Platoons of B.Coy paraded at 9am to continue wiring under RE. Remainder of Battalion employed improving trenches and shelter and taking down huts in camp. C.27.b.15. C.O. Adjutant and Company commanders go forward in morning to reconnoitre frontline system.	
	19th		Advanced party of Intelligence and Signal officers, 1 Officer from each company and 1 NCO from each platoon go forward to take over front line from 9th Royal Inniskillings, Wednesday 2pm. Ration Strength 15 Officers OR 510 SP 23 OR 734	

WAR DIARY or INTELLIGENCE SUMMARY

Army Form C. 2118.

Place	Date	Hour	Summary of Events and Information	Remarks and references to Appendices
FRONT LINE	19/20		The Battalion marched out of camp at 8.15 P.M. Scouts and Battle zone taken over by 2nd Royal Inniskilling Fusiliers. The relief of the 9th R. Innis. drilling Fusiliers is reported complete at 11 P.M. Dispositions of companies as follows. A Coy. 1 Platoon SPREE FM C18d 35.35 1 Platoon C 24 a 10.85 1 Platoon C 24 a 35.60. 1 Platoon Coy Hd Qrs C23b95.20 B Coy. 1 Platoon WINE HO. C18c 80.80 1 Platoon C17d 85.40. 1 Platoon CHEDDAR VILLA C21a 70.95. 1 Platoon of Coy Hd Qrs BOSSAERT KEEP C23b 30.35 C Coy. 1 Platoon C23c 35.20 Afterwards moved to VON HUGEL FM C23d 10.60. 2 Platoons and Coy HdQrs PICKEL HAUBE KEEP C.23c 60.70. 1 Platoon C 23 a C0.20. D Coy. in WIELTJE Dugout C28b 25.55 to man WIELTJE defences if necessary. 1 Platoon B22d 30.00. 1 Platoon C 28b 75.85 1 Platoon C28b 70.60. 1 Platoon C 28 b 26.65. Batln. Hd Qrs WIELTJE DUGOUT C28b 80.75 A Patrol of 1 Officer and Bomber left our lines at SPREE FM C18d 35.35 at midnight and found dugout at C18d 30.30 un-occupied, also dugouts C24a 9.8. and C24 & 15.65. Patrol returned to our lines by track 5 at 2AM. Machine guns were faintly active during the night.	
	20/21		Enemy artillery quiet. A patrol of 1 officer, 2 SOR left our lines by track 6 at 11 P.M. they found WINE HO C18c 80.95 unoccupied; they then proceeded to enemy's Pill Box at C18d 20.95	

WAR DIARY or INTELLIGENCE SUMMARY.

Army Form C. 2118.

(Erase heading not required.)

Instructions regarding War Diaries and Intelligence Summaries are contained in F. S. Regs., Part II. and the Staff Manual respectively. Title pages will be prepared in manuscript.

Place	Date	Hour	Summary of Events and Information	Remarks and references to Appendices
FRONT LINE	21/22		Out were observed and fired on and could not approach nearer to bright moonlight. Patrol returned to our lines at 2.30 AM. Day enlivened by previous WELTJE dinner. Enemy artillery was active against WIELTJE dugouts at ODDAVILLA C23d 30.35 at 8.30 PM and BESSAERT C23d 30.35 at 8.35PM. Enemy aircraft showed increased activity. Planes were observed over our lines and engaged with MGs frequently. A patrol of 2 officers 30 OR left our lines at 6.15 a 4575 and west of dugouts near BORDER HO C18c 18. They occupied unoccupied Patrol returned to front at 1.15 am.	
	22/23		Enemy artillery active against WIELTJE during Thursday about 6 gas shells fell them in Hammering. 1 man sent to hospital with gas poisoning. The night was too bright for a large fighting patrol 1 officer 5 OR left WIELTJE No C18c 89 and occupied a dug out at about C18d 10.95 the Bosh threw bombs at them and opened machine gun fire from about E.18 b 10.85 Patrol returned at 1.15AM by point of road C Company moved 1 Platoon from C23c 4.2 to Pill Box C23c 85.40. Day event up 1 Platoon to C23d 15.20 This platoon to be under the orders of OC Coy. During this time on the line all companies were at work improving their positions and wire. C Coy erected a new switch built of wire from C23d 26.20 to B.50 S.4 AERT to conform with the line of resistance.	
	23/24		Enemy artillery still very quiet. A patrol of 2 officers 20 OR went out from SPREEFM at 3 AM to obtain and identification of the Enemy in front of Brook was seen. Patrol worked around them in two parties but a man from SPREEFM opened fire and they ran away. Ground was thoroughly searched but no trace could found. Patrol returned	

WAR DIARY
or
INTELLIGENCE SUMMARY.
(Erase heading not required.)

Army Form C. 2118.

Place	Date	Hour	Summary of Events and Information	Remarks and references to Appendices
	25/26		Enemy artillery again very quiet. The Battalion is relieved by the 2nd Royal Irish Rifles in support and proceeds to IRISH FARM Camp when it becomes Battalion in support and is under orders to be ready to man the Battle Zone. Relief complete reported by 23.53.	Vide BO 83.
IRISH FM CAMP	26th		A and D Coys find working party of 2 Platoons at 10 am relieved by other 2 Platoons at 1pm to work salvaging & material.	
CANAL BANK	26/27		Battalion moves to CANAL BANK march off midnight. All companies reported in by 3.5 AM.	Vide Brigade 84
			Brigade dispositions — Bridges 2 inclusive — Dispositions C Coy East Bank M68 — C25 d 73. Vide Map Attached.
			D Coy East Bank C25 d 73 to C25 a 96 fly. West Bank 116 59 to C25 d 1.6 Bn. West Bank C25 d 16 - C25 b7.	
			Head Quarters C25 d 20. The Battalion is accommodated in dugouts and ?? to man the defences on bank with 18 BN Rifles on left and 20th Durham? on right. During heavy shelling with S.G. All companies at work on their defences. Draft of 98 O.R. from 30 B reports on 29th. Inst. 18 from A Coy MP Hoyd Lodwick 2nd Lt Hin Dunean. B sheet B1 W W?? C. 2 Lieut W Hodgson about A.3 H approach about 9 R? Newton. O about R/E Benham. B. 2Lieut C W Vernon C.	
	27 - 29		B Company sent up to IRISH FARM in support to 2nd R Innis. during 29 ??.	
	30th		Work continued. Draft of 47 OR arrives.	

Signed ?? Lt Col
Comdg 1st Bn N. Lanc?? ??

WAR DIARY
INTELLIGENCE SUMMARY

Army Form C. 2118.

Volume 38.

Place	Date	Hour	Summary of Events and Information	Remarks and references to Appendices
CANAL BANK.	April 1st–4th		Companies at work on their defences. Salvage parties collected shells etc. Advanced party of 1 officer from each company 1 NCO from each platoon goes forward to take over the front line from 9th R Inniskilling Fusiliers. One O/R officer per Coy and 1 NCO per Platoon go forward to take over the front line.	Vide Defence Scheme for CANAL BANK Rg moving attack Vol 37.
FRONT LINE	5/4		Battalion proceeds to take over the front line system from 9th Bn Royal Inniskilling Fusiliers. Relief complete reported at 1.5 AM.	Vide Bn Ord No 85. Private Order No 27.
	6/4		Disposition: A Coy left front Coy. B Coy Reserve Coy C Coy Right Front Coy. D Coy Centre front Coy. Vide attd map.	Vide attd map.
		6 pm	Enemy artillery active. St JEAN heavily shelled with 5.9. Considerable movement behind enemy lines reported from our OP. Occasional anti fire from JASPER FM on Picket heads. Three patrols left our line. 2 from left company to work in conjunction against enemy post reported at C2.a.9.9. These patrols consisted of 1 officer 15 OR each. They visited the supposed post but encountered no enemy. Another patrol went out from night company and visited C9.4.? FM which was found unoccupied. The wire round the farm is thick and unbroken. Farewell letter from Maj Gen Nugent received, copy attached.	acd. Defence Scheme
	7/6.		Enemy artillery again active. WIELTJE area shelled at 10 AM 2 PM and 4:30 PM with 5.9. and 17 mm. C2.2.b.90.30 was shelled with 5.9. from 2 PM to 6:30 PM from direction of ZONNEBEKE	

Army Form C. 2118.

WAR DIARY
or
INTELLIGENCE SUMMARY.
(Erase heading not required.)

Place	Date	Hour	Summary of Events and Information	Remarks and references to Appendices
	8/9		Enemy Aircraft showed increased activity during the afternoon. The Snipers that had been firing from JASPER Fm were silenced by our snipping and Lewis Gun fire. Very little enemy shelling toward known times. A Patrol of 1 officer 7 OR left our lines at C23c30.90 and visited Pill Box at C23b20.30. It was found unoccupied and showed no signs of having been used as a listening post as had been thought. Patrol returned to point of exit at 1.30 AM. A Patrol of 1 officer 8 OR left our lines at C23c9.6 at 10 PM and went to C23d10.80 to lie in wait for Boat moving to and from JASPER. No enemy were seen. Our Artillery active all day. Enemy also fairly active. WIELTJE was very heavily shelled with 5.9s from ZONNEBEKE direction at 10.45 - 11.15 AM, 2.30 PM, and 4.30 PM. At 11.15 AM an enemy plane of new type flew very low over our lines and stayed for some time. A patrol left our lines at C23c6.7 and went to C23d9.9 returning at 1.15 AM. The enemy was encountered. Another patrol of 1 officer 8 OR	
	9/9		left our lines at C23a 4.3 and went along track 6 to C23b10.75. No enemy was encountered. Patrol returned by point of exit at 1.45 AM. Observers saw enemy working on TM emplacement at BRIDGE Ho. Our Artillery active all day. Enemy artillery quiet in morning. C Battery 153 did a good shot on TM emplacement observed hurriedly at 2 PM. 6 inch Hows opened on it and Bosch were seen	

WAR DIARY or INTELLIGENCE SUMMARY

Army Form C. 2118.

Place	Date	Hour	Summary of Events and Information	Remarks and references to Appendices
			running. They returned just before dawn and rejoined their Tm. Our Snipers were active. Two hits were registered. A patrol of 1 officer 12 OR left our lines at I.23.a.45.20 at 10 pm and went to C.23.b.05.80. to try and catch stragglers from relief. They Bosh were seen approaching along track. They turned off into some huts about C.23.a.85.75. Another party of 3 followed them. A very light disclosed a working party of about 30 working near these huts. Patrol returned to point of exit at 12.30 am and another patrol of 1 officer 12 OR went out to same spot returning at 2.30 am without seeing any enemy. Another patrol left our lines at C.23.c.66 at 10 pm and went to C.23.c.45.10 along railway line. Enemy could be heard working on RAT F.M. but our artillery was firing on it. Patrol returned to our lines about 12.30 am and another patrol of 1 officer 8 OR went out to same point without encountering enemy. Ahead of 1 officer 12 OR left our lines at C.29.a.30.70 and went to C.23.b.90.20. No enemy was seen and patrol returned at 1.30 am.	
	10/11		Enemy artillery fairly active. HILLTOP shelled with 4.20 at 11am. The Battalion is relieved by 1st Bn the Royal Irish Rifles and proceeds to BRIELEN and TROIS TOURS. Relief complete 1.15 am. B.Bs and C.Coys BRIELEN. A.Coy TROIS TOURS. HdQrs in TROIS TOURS Château.	Vide App Bat Instruction No. 28. Vide App Order No. 68. Vide App Bat Bat Order No. 27.
	11-12th		Battalion resting and cleaning up. 5 pm 13th Winds came from transport lines and details for quiet tour in the line are sent down.	

Army Form C. 2118.

WAR DIARY
or
INTELLIGENCE SUMMARY.
(Erase heading not required.)

Place	Date	Hour	Summary of Events and Information	Remarks and references to Appendices
CANAL BANK	14th		Battalion moves to CANAL BANK and becomes battalion in support to 9th Royal Inniskillings, Fusrs on the Line. March off first company 9pm. Batty reported complete 11.45 PM. Disp: as in	Vide Bn Order Nos 88 89
	15th		Acompany C21 a 2.6. Bcompany C21 b 7.9 Ccompany 11 B 8.2. Dcompany. KA 21 E 12.a.2.8. Vide att. Order
	16 - 18th		Company moves forward to WILSONS Fm. C 26 b 32. Company moves forward to WILSONS Fm. C 26 b 32. Company at work improving their defences. 17th Fifteen per company and 1 NCO per platoon go forward to reconnoitre the front line.	
	2/9/17		The Battalion relieves the 9th Bn 11th Royal Inniskillings Fus in the front line system. Rly reported complete 12.30 AM. Dispositions. Bcompany Rly front Company. Ccompany centre front company. D company right front company. Astrol of 1 officer 60R officer man at C28 d 30.20 at 11 PM and went along light railway to MILL at F56.25.80 which was found deserted patrol then proceeded to NEW at F51 30.70 which was also deserted. Patrol then returned to own lines at 14.30.40. Another patrol of 3 officers 50R of our lines at C29 e 30.16 at 1AM and went to WARWICK Fm which was found unoccupied. Patrol then went forward towards PILL BOX at C29 e 55.35 which was found occupied of A Boche man and towards Islandand Fm. Patrol laid on them for sometime from the PILL BOX and Patrol returned and returned to own lines at C29 c 10.30.	Vide Bn Order No 90

Army Form C. 2118.

WAR DIARY
or
INTELLIGENCE SUMMARY.
(Erase heading not required.)

Instructions regarding War Diaries and Intelligence Summaries are contained in F. S. Regs., Part II. and the Staff Manual respectively. Title pages will be prepared in manuscript.

Place	Date	Hour	Summary of Events and Information	Remarks and references to Appendices
FRONT LINE	19/20.		Enemy artillery quiet. Two patrols went out from our lines during the night. 1st Patrol of Officer 20 O.R. left our lines at PROWSE FM C28d 40.20. and went along light railway to MILL COT and NEW COT. Thence on to (ROMP FM where a PILL BOX and some huts were found unoccupied. Patrol went on in direction of the STABLES where a thick belt of wire prevented entry. a TM was firing from a point East of THE STABLES onto MILL COT. Heavy transport was heard on the YPRES ZONNEBEKE Road. Another patrol of 2 Officers 21 other ranks left our lines at C29 c 10.25 at 1.35 am and to try and secure an identification from PILL BOX at C29 c 50.55. Patrol was unable to secure the identification owing to enemy firing a light TM and MG fire on them from the PILL BOX at C29 c 50.55.	Vide Bn Order 91
	20/21		Enemy artillery fairly active. The 9080 was shelled with 5.9s from 8.20am to 12 noon. Disposition as attend. 2 Companies in front line. D Coy Right front B Company left front. C Company counter attack A Company reserve. Original posts in front line of C Company taken over by B and D. Stakes over hut at C28d 90.25 Stakes over hut at C28d 60.20. 2 Patrols out on our front during the night. 1st Patrol Officer lines C28d 55 at 1AM and proceeded afterwards to PILL Box at C29 c 50.55. The ground was found so marshy that the	Vide attd Mss.

WAR DIARY
or
INTELLIGENCE SUMMARY

Army Form C. 2118.

(Erase heading not required.)

Place	Date	Hour	Summary of Events and Information	Remarks and references to Appendices
	21/22nd		enemy patrol approach was down the light railway at C29 c 60.30. This approach was covered with M.G. and T.M. approach down. Trench at C29 c 60.00 was found impassable. Patrol returned to point of exit at 2:45 am. Another patrol left our lines at C28 d 40.20 and reconnoitered east went to CRUMP PM. 1 officer and 10 O.R. approaching S remained at NEW COT on covering party while 1 offr and 10 O.R. took up a position E of (from PFM. when they lay out. Patrol encountered no enemy and returned hour from at 2 AM. Except for a bombardment of our line in C 28 d and OXFORD ROAD with Heavy TM at 4.20 AM 21st the enemy was quiet. Our 4.5 Hows replied to this bombardment and during the day 153rd Batty did a shoot on Pill Box at C29 d 60.35 With an 18 inch hit. A patrol left our lines at C28 d 3.2 at 11.10 PM and went to E5 a 80.90. When they lay in wait (visid VPRES ZONNEBEKE ROAD. No enemy were seen and patrol returned at 1.30 AM.	No. 92.
	22/23rd		The day passed quietly in the evening the Battalion was relieved by 2nd Royal Inniskilling V.U. Battalion situation and proceeded to BRIELEN and TROIS TOURS. Relief complete at 1.45	the Officer's Sund for Regin Sqdron

Army Form C. 2118.

WAR DIARY
or
INTELLIGENCE SUMMARY.
(Erase heading not required.)

Instructions regarding War Diaries and Intelligence Summaries are contained in F. S. Regs., Part II. and the Staff Manual respectively. Title pages will be prepared in manuscript.

Place	Date	Hour	Summary of Events and Information	Remarks and references to Appendices
BRIELEN.	23rd to 26th		The Battalion Rests and became up. Companies inspected by the Commanding Officer.	Vide Scheme for Defence of River System. Vide Map shown. Dispositions
CANAL BANK.	26/27		The Battalion relieves the 9th R Innis Skilling Fusrs in the CANAL BANK and becomes Support Battalion. Heavy Gas shelling from 2AM to 4AM during attack on the trench at DICKEBUSH LAKE. Gas Masks worn for 2 hours. 2 Men sent to hospital with gas poisoning.	
	28-30		Companies employed wiring and improving defences.	

SECRET.

1ST BATTALION THE ROYAL INNISKILLING FUSILIERS ORDER No.78.

3/4/18

Reference Map:- HAZEBROU CK.5A.

1. The Battalion will move to ROUSBRUGGE today, entraining at MOINCOURT at 2200 hours.

2. 1st. Line Transport will accompany the Battalion.

3. The Battalion will parade on the Field opposite Orderly Room ready to march off at 2230 hours.

4. Dress:- Marching Order, with caps(if possible) Blankets will be carried on the man.

(Sd) D.H.F.Davidson. 2/Lieut. & A/Adjt.
1st. Battalion The Royal Inniskilling Fusiliers.

Copies to:-
    1 & 2.Staff.
    3 & 4.War Diary.
    5 6 7 & 8.Companies.
    9. QR.MR.
    10. T.O.
    11. M.O.
    12. File.

S E C R E T.

ADMINISTRATIVE ORDER TO ACCOMPANY BATTALION ORDER NO-78.

1. The Battalion will entrain at MOINCOURT at 2200.

2. All personnel will be at entraining point at 2100.

3. Transport will accompany Battalion and will entrain full.

4. Supply wagons and Transport will be at ENTRAINING point at 1900.

5. Rations will be taken on the train for consumption on the day after entraining.

6. Officers Kits and surplus stores will be dumped at Qr.Mr's Stores at 1600.

7. All billets will be left clean and ready for inspection by 8.30.p.m.

(sd) D.N.F.Davidson. 2/Lieut.& A/Adjt.
1st. Battalion The Royal Inniskilling Fusiliers.

Copies to :-
All recipients of Bn.Order No 78.

SECRET.

1ST BATTALION THE ROYAL INNISKILLING FUSILIERS ORDER NO.78.

5th. APRIL 1918.

1. The Battalion will move to the CANAL Bank and Battle Zone tomorrow.

2. Advanced Party, C.Q.M.Ss and Sgt. McKinney under Lt. D.N.F. Davidson will be ready to move at an hour to be notified later.

3. Instruction for move and details of dispositions will be notified later.

Cunningham
Capt & Adjt.
1st. Bn. The Royal Inniskilling Fusiliers.

Copies to:-
1 & 2. Staff.
3 & 4. War Diary.
5.6.7 & 8. Companies.
9. Qr. Mr.
10. T.O.

SECRET.

CONTINUATION OF BATTALION ORDER NO. 72.

6th. April 1918

1. The Battalion will Parade at 1.20.p.m., to proceed to the Support Area, CANAL BANK.
    Dress:- Marching Order, Steel Helmets. One Blanket will be carried on the man.

2. ROUTE:- HOSPITAL FARM   B.20.b.3.7.
              B.20.d.4.8.   B.22.c.5.3.
              BRIELAN.   B.30.a.8.2.
              CANAL BANK where guides will meet them.
    A distance of 100 yards will be observed between Companies and groups of six vehicles.

3. Kits:- All Kits will be ready by 11.0.a.m. and stacked at Quartermaster's Stores.

7. Dinners will be served at 12.noon.

8. Completion of relief will be reported to Battalion Hd. Qrs.

9. The Camp will be left clean and in a sanitary condition.

10. Transport and Quartermaster's Stores will be accommodated in SIEGE CAMP when it has been vacated.

(Sd) G. F. Framingham. Capt & Adjt.
1st. Battalion The Royal Inniskilling Fusiliers.

Copies to

    1 & 2. Staff.
    3 & 4. War Diary.
    5 6 7 & 8. Companies.
    9. Qr. Mr.
    10. T.O.
    11. M.O.
    12. File.

SECRET.   Copy No." ".

1ST BATTALION THE ROYAL INNISKILLING FUSILIERS ORDER NO. 30.

11th. APRIL 1918.

Reference Map:- E.3. 1/10.000.

1. The 1st. Royal Inniskilling Fusiliers will relieve the 2nd. Royal Irish Rifles in the Front Line, Left Sub-sector on the night of the 12/13th. inst.
   Battalion Headquarters NORFOLK HOUSE.

2. The Relief will be carried out as follows:-
   "C" Co. 1st. R. Innis. Fus., will relieve "C" Co. 2/R. Irish Rifles.
   "D" Co.   "   "   "   "   "   "B" Co.   "   "   "
   "A" Co.   "   "   "   "   "   "A" Co.   "   "   "
   "B" Co.   "   "   "   "   "   "D" Co.   "   "   "
   Dress:- Marching Order without blanket, 1 day's rations will be carried.

3. "C" & "D" & Hd. Qr. Companies will proceed by Train, details will be issued later.
   "A" & "B" Companies will proceed by march route via GLOSTER AVENUE, but will not cross the STEENBEEK before 8.15.p.m. An interval of 25 yards will be observed between Platoons.

4. One guide per Platoon and one for Company Headquarters will meet the Companies detraining at BROOKLYN at 7.30.p.m.
   Guides for the Companies marching will meet them at the junction of the duckboard track and POELCAPELLE Road in U.30.d. They will be at this point at 8.30.p.m.
   The Marching Companies will reconnitre the track by day.

5. O.C. Companies will send an Officer to REGINA CROSS at 10.0.a.m. tomorrow 12th. inst to point out the Company Sectors of the Battalion Battle zone to representatives of 2/R.I.Rs.

6. Receipts for all Trench stores taken over will be forwarded to Battalion Headquarters.

7. Completion of Relief will be reported to Bn. Hd. Qrs. by code word RIGHT.

                                                    Capt & Adjt.
                                        1st. Bn. The Royal Inniskilling Fusiliers.

Copies to
   1 & 2. Staff.
   3 & 4. War Diary.
   5. 6. 7. 8. Companies.
   9. Qr. Mr.

SECRET.

ADMINISTRATIVE ORDER TO ACCOMPANY BATTALION ORDER NO.80.

11th. April 1918.

I. **RATIONS.-** One day's rations will be carried on the man. On each subsequent night rations will be brought up by limbers to RETOUR CROSS ROADS. They will arrive about 8.30.p.m. O.C. "B"Company will detail the necessary carrying parties for the Companies forward and C.Q.M.Ss. will see rations and water delivered to their Coys., The rations of "B"Company will be off loaded at DELTA FARM. A water cart and three soyer stoves will be at PHEASANT TRENCH.

O.C.Companies will detail a guide to be at the cross roads every night by 8.30.p.m.

OFFICERS KITS.- All Officers Kits will be removed to Transport Lines by G.S. Wagons at 10.a.m. tomorrow 12th.inst.

BLANKETS.- The Blankets of "A" & "B" Companies will be removed at 10.a.m. and of Hd.Qr.Coy., "C" & "D" Companies at 1.0.p.m. They will be rolled in bundles of 10 properly labelled and stacked at a convenient place for the wagons to pick them up. Companies will arrange loading parties.

TRANSPORT.- A Limber will take the Lewis Guns of "A" & "B" Companies to RETOUR CROSS ROADS at 6.0.p.m. 1 man of each of these Companies will accompany this Limber. The O.C.Companies will arrange to collect them from RETOUR CROSS ROADS.

A Limber will collect the Orderly Room Boxes, Officers Mess Stores and Medical Stores at 5.30.p.m., and convey to Transport Lines.

LEWIS GUN MAGAZINES.- 48 magazines per Company will be taken into the Line.

PERSONNEL.- O.C.Companies will arrange for a percentage of all specialists, Lewis Gunners Scouts, Snipers, Signallers and Instructors to remain behind, also 1 Sergeant, 1 Corporal and Company Clerk. Officers and N.C.O's and men for courses will be accommodated at SIEGE CAMP.

All details not proceeding forward will report at the Transport Lines SIEGE CAMP by 3.0.p.m.

PUBLIC MONEY.- No Public Money or Company Records will be taken forward.

RUNNERS.- On completion of Relief each Company will send a runner to report and remain at Battalion Headquarters.

SANITARY.- All dugouts and area to be left in a clean and sanitary condition.

Sgt. Bardill and Pioneers will clear up after the Bn., leaves will then report to SIEGE CAMP.

RECEIPTS.- Receipts for all stores handed over in the Battle Zone will be forwarded to Battalion Headquarters.

(Sd) G. E. Framingham. Capt & Adjt.
1st.Battalion The Royal Inniskilling Fusiliers.

Copies to
All recipients of Bn. Order No.80

S E C R E T.   Copy No.

1ST BATTALION THE ROYAL INNISKILLING FUSILIERS ORDER NO. 81.

15th. APRIL 1918.

Reference Map. B. 3. 1/10.000. 28. N.W. 2.

1.   The Battalion will withdraw from the Outpost Line gradually tonight, through the Battalion in the Battle Zone, leaving a skeleton line to cover the movement and will go into Brigade reserve in IRISH FARM CAMP.

2.   "A" COMPANY.
        At 9.30.p.m., O.C."A"Company will withdraw his Company by Platoons via GROUSE AVENUE destroying the Track up to the STEENBEEK and GLOSTER AVENUE from TRIANGLE LANGEMARK ROAD to STEENBEEK. After destroying tracks he will proceed direct to CAMP via TRIANGLE - REGINA CROSS - HAMMOND CROSS.

        "B" COMPANY.
        At 9.30.p.m., O.C."B"Company will withdraw 2 Platoons via POELCAPELLE - TRIANGLE - REGINA CROSS - CAMP.
        These 2 Platoons will destroy camouflage screens on the way, and GLOSTER AVENUE from U.30.d.5.8. - U.29.d.8.1.
        He will place two Platoons, one at DELTA with a post on main road N.E. of RETOUR CROSS ROADS, and one at Junction of GLOSTER AVENUE and main road, to cover withdrawal of skeleton outposts along main road. These two Platoons will be responsible for making barricades on main road. They will not withdraw until further orders.

        "C" & "D" Companies.
        At 2.0.a.m., 16th.inst., O.C."C" & "D"Companies will withdraw 3 Sections per Platoon from the Outpost line and proceed via GROUSE AVENUE - NORFOLK HOUSE - RETOUR CROSS ROADS - REGINA CROSS - CAMP, & GLOSTER AVENUE - REGINA CROSS - CAMP respectively. "D"Company will be responsible for damaging track from V.19.d.5.0. to main POELCAPELLE ROAD.
        At 4.0.a.m., O.C."C" & "D"Companies will withdraw outposts via GROUSE AVENUE - RETOUR CROSS ROADS and GLOSTER AVENUE & RETOUR CROSS ROADS and proceed via REGINA CROSS to CAMP keeping one Section each as rear guard and smashing remainder of tracks.
        At 3.45.a.m. 16th., Bn.Hd.Qrs., will move to U.30.d.5.8., and withdraw to Camp as soon as Skeleton outposts have passed.

3.   As soon as Skeleton Outposts have passed through 2 Platoons of "B"Company orders will be given for "B"Company to withdraw to Camp via REGINA CROSS. O.C."B"Company will keep Platoon at DELTA as rearguard.

4.   Control Posts will be placed at TRIANGLE.

5.   All troops must be WEST of STEENBEEK by 5.45.a.m., 16th.inst.

                    (Sd) G. E. Framingham. Captain.
                    1st. Battalion The Royal Inniskilling Fusiliers.
Issued at 2.0.p.m.
        Copies to
                1 & 2. War Diary.
                3 & 4. Staff.
                5, 6, 7 & 8. Companies.
                9. M.O.

S E C R E T.   Copy No. " ".

1ST-BATTALION THE ROYAL INNISKILLING FUSILIERS ORDER NO.82.

19th. April 1918.

1. The 1st. Battalion The Royal Inniskilling Fusiliers will relieve the 9th. Battalion Royal Inniskilling Fusiliers on the night of the 19/20th. inst.

2. "A" Company 1st. R. Innis. Fus., will relieve "A" Company 9th. R. Innis. Fus.
   "B"   "   "   "   "   "   "   "B"   "   "   "   "   "
   "C"   "   "   "   "   "   "   "C"   "   "   "   "   "
   "D"   "   "   "   "   "   "   "D"   "   "   "   "   "

   Order of March:-
   Advance Platoon "A" Company will move off at 8.0.p.m.
      "   "   "B"   "   . A. B. C. D.
   25 yards interval between Platoons.
   One day's ration will be carried on the man.
   Dress:- Marching Order.

3. One guide for each Platoon and one Guide for Company Hd. Qrs., will meet Platoons at Battalion Headquarters at Road junction WEILTJE.

4. Receipts for all trench stores taken over will be sent to Battalion Headquarters by 10.0.a.m. on 20th. inst.

5. Work in forward area will be carefully taken over.

6. Completion of Relief will be reported to Battalion Headquarters by the name of the Company Commander.

7. ACKNOWLEDGE.

                    (Sd) R. W. W. Stephenson. 2/Lieut.& Adjt.
                    1st. Battalion The Royal Inniskilling Fusiliers.

Copies to
    1. Commanding Officer.
    2. War Diary.
    3. "   " .
    4. 5. 6 & 7. Companies.
    8. I. T. R.
    9. Qr. Mr.
    10. File.

SECRET.   Copy No. " 1"

1ST BATTALION THE ROYAL INNISKILLING FUSILIERS ORDER NO. 83.

25th. APRIL 1918.

1.   The 2nd. Battalion Royal Inniskilling Fusiliers will relieve
1st. Battalion The Royal Inniskilling Fusiliers on the night of the
25/26th. inst.
     "A" Company 2nd. R. Innis. Fus. will relieve "A" Company 1st. R. Innis. Fus.
     "B"   "   "   "   "   "   "   "   "B"   "   "   "   "   "
     "D"   "   "   "   "   "   "   "   "C"   "   "   "   "   "
     "C"   "   "   "   "   "   "   "   "D"   "   "   "   "   "
     On completion of Relief the Battalion will move into Billets
vacated by the 2nd. Battalion Royal Inniskilling Fusiliers. The Bn.,
will then be in Brigade Support.
     C.Q.M.Ss. will take over billets from the correcponding Companies
of the 2nd. Battalion Royal Inniskilling Fusiliers.

2.   One guide per Platoon and one guide per Company Headquarters will
report to Battalion Headquarters at 6.0.p.m. Not more than two guides
at a time to leave forward Company Headquarters.

3.   All Trench Stores, Maps etc., will be handed over and receipts
forwarded to Battalion Headquarters by 10.0.a.m. 26th. inst.

4.   Trench Kits, Cooking Utensils, Salvage etc., will be dumped by 8.0.p.m.
on the SPREE FARM - WIELTJE ROAD where Transport can collect. One
man per Company will remain with kits, and accompany limbers to IRISH
FARM.

5.   Lewis Guns and ammunition will be carried.

6.   Officers Kits and blankets will be sent up from Transport Lines
to IRISH FARM.

7.   The completion of Relief will be reported to Battalion Headquarters
by the surname of O.C. Company.

8.   ACKNOWLEDGE.

                         (Sd) R.W.W. Stephenson. 2/Lieut & Adjt.
                    1st. Battalion The Royal Inniskilling Fusiliers.
Copies to:-
         1. Commanding Officer.
         2. Second in Command.
         3 & 4. War Diary.
         5. 6. 7 & 8. Companies.
         9. Qr. Mr.
        10. I.T.U.
        11. File.

SECRET.   Copy No. " ".

1ST BATTALION THE ROYAL INNISKILLING FUSILIERS ORDER NO. 84.

                                                    26th. April 1918.

Reference Map Sheet 28.N.W., Ed.6B. 1/20.000.

1. The following dispositions will be taken up on the night of the
   26/27th.inst.
      The Battalion will move back to the CANAL BANK and be in BRIGADE
   SUPPORT.
      "C" & "D" Companies will be on the EAST bank of the CANAL.
      "A" & "B" Companies will be on the WEST Bank of the CANAL.
      Battalion Headquarters will be on the WEST bank of the CANAL.

2. TOOLS   "A" "B" & "C" Companies will carry tools. Tools can be drawn
   from the dump close to Headquarters Mess.

3. ORDER OF MARCH.   Headquarters "C" "D" "A" & "B".
   Headquarters to pass starting point (Level crossing C.27.a.3.8.)
   at 12.15.a.m. 100 yards interval to be maintained between Platoons.
      ROUTE   Level Crossing to Railway Bridge Canal.

4. O.C. Companies will report by Runner to Battalion Headquarters when
   their Companies are complete in new positions.

5. ACKNOWLEDGE.

              (Sd) R.W.W.Stephenson. 2/Lieut.& Adjutant.
            1st. Battalion The Royal Inniskilling Fusiliers.

Copies to.
          1. Commanding Officer.
          2 & 3. War Diary.
          4 5 6 & 7. Companies.
          8. 2/ Command.

To
O.C. "A" Company.
　　 "B" Company.
　　 "C" Company.
　　 "D" Company.
　　 Quartermaster.
　　 Transport Officer.

　　　　　　On receipt of orders to "MAN BATTLE ZONE" Companies will immediately proceed to the positions temporarily allotted as under:-

"A" Company.　　Hd.Qrs. & 2 Platoons. JULIET FARM. 1 Platoon C.II. Central. 1 Platoon at HUGEL HALLES.

"B" Company.　　Hd.Qrs. & 1 Platoon at C.II.a.0.7. 1 Platoon FERDINAND FARM, 1 Platoon Trench C.11.a.4.5. 1 Platoon Trench C.11.a.7.5.

"C" Company.　　Hd.Qrs. & 3 Platoons at BOSCASTLE TRENCH. 1 Platoon at VAR VARDAR.

"D" Company.　　Hd.Qrs. & 2 Platoons at RACECOURSE FARM. 1 Platoon ENGLISH TREES. 1 Platoon OBLONG FARM.

Battalion Headquarters will be in BOSCASTLE TRENCH near the Road.

　　　　　　The Quartermaster will arrange for Transport to remove all stores of Companies and Battalion Headquarters; and the Administrative Section, vide Table in S.S.145 of Battalion and Companies.

　　　　　　The Officer i/c of Signallers will arrange to leave behind 33% of the Signallers and O.C.Companies a proportion of their Lewis Gunners and Instructors, they will proceed to the Transport Lines with the Battalion Administrative Section.

　　　　　　Companies will proceed to their locations as rapidly as possible reporting to Battalion Headquarters when they are in position.

　　　　　　O.C. Companies will ensure that every man has a full water bottle and iron rations complete.

　　　　　　Companies will move to their positions in a suitable formation, the necessary distances being observed between Platoons.

　　　　　　The position of all Companies and their functions will be explained to all N.C.O's.

　　　　　　Dress:- Fighting Order.

ST JULIEN 28 NW 2. Path of attacks C25 1,1 Scale 1:5,000.

REFERENCES:
Lewis Posts.
Machine Guns.
Lewis Gun Posts at end of Battery.
Sap or Old Emplacements.

Work Completed.
Work to be Completed.

SHEET 28 NW2 ST JULIEN Parts of squares. C.17,18. 22,23,24. 28,29.   Scale 1:10,000

The two standing Patrols of 1 Platoon each at SPREE FM and WINE Ho are found by the night and left Coy companies respectively of the support company two platoons attached from the main company.

○ Platoons
○○ Companies
▭ Bat⁴ⁿ HQ
▭ Coy HQ

Posts of 1 section
Held by night only

X.36

Miss Harris

Nov 28

1ST ROYAL INNISKILLING FUSILIERS.

WAR DIARY

FOR MONTH OF MAY, 1918.

Army Form C. 2118.

WAR DIARY
or
INTELLIGENCE SUMMARY.
(Erase heading not required.)

Place	Date	Hour	Summary of Events and Information	Remarks and references to Appendices
CANAL BANK	30		Battalion relieve 9th Bn R Inniskillings in line. A+C front line, B+D Support Bn	Op. No 93. H/F Disposn
			Reserve.	
		10:30	Patrol 2/Lt W Hamilton + 16 O.R. left our lines at PROWSE F.M. Object. To reconnoitre MILL + NEW COTT and around S of WARWICK F.M. to visit WARWICK F.M. and obtain an identification if possible. Result: No. began of enemy in MILL + NEW COTT. From there sounds of digging was heard from direction of CRUMP F.M. Our artillery fired and then ceased firing on target. Patrol then proceeded to visit WARWICK F.M. when about 30' from what appeared to be the remains of a pillbox C.29.c.6.2. The patrol was challenged and fired on. Fire was returned and the pillbox was rushed from two sides and bombed. Two Germans were killed, one being an N.C.O., two escaped and four were captured. Patrol then returned, being fired on by a M.G. in vicinity of C.29.c.75.25. Route Light Railway from PROWSE F.M. to MILL COTT, main Road to OXFORD RD along OXFORD RD to +Trk and thence to WARWICK F.M. returning by main road by front of enemy. Casualties 4 O.R. Missing and returned 1 a.m. 31st T4 + 25.35.	
		12:0	Patrol 2/Lt Legg + 12 O.R. left our lines. Object: To examine hub and pillboxes in vicinity of C.29.a.6.3. and discover hostile posts in that vicinity, also to obtain identification if possible. Result: The most northerly hub was examined and found unoccupied. Patrol then proceeded along buried cable as far as old trench C.29.a.55.66. and lay in wait + listened. In about 10 min. two Germans approached patrol from an easterly direction. On reaching the old trench one came forward the other remaining near the trench about 40' from patrol fired on them in error, the nearer + one was slightly wounded and captured. The other ran away. Patrol then returned to front of exit trench, thence NE along buried cable to Caliban trench, along old line of trench and for information obtained Wounded prisoner C. 2113/13 prisoners Sec	

A 5834 Wt W4973/M687 750,000 8/16 D.D.&L. Ltd Form C. 2118/13.

WAR DIARY
or
INTELLIGENCE SUMMARY.
(Erase heading not required.)

Army Form C. 2118.

Place	Date	Hour	Summary of Events and Information	Remarks and references to Appendices
	30/5/18		Both our hostile artillery moderately active; observation was good + a [?] amount of enemy movement was observed.	
	31/5/18	10.40pm	Patrol. 2/Lt. Brabson and 12 O.R. left our lines C.29.c.20.55. Object: To locate enemy posts in neighbourhood of C.29.c.55.50 and observe and report on nature of hostile known to exist there. Result. A sentry was observed standing outside shelter at C.29.c.55.62. Another man was seen walking up and down between the shelter and the shelter at C.29.c.55.60. He put up Very lights at intervals. A wiring party of about 8 men was observed putting up Very lights for C.29.c.60.58. Many Very lights went up from WARWICK FM. Route: Along old trench to Pill-box at C.29.c.50.60. + returning by same route. entering our lines at C.29.c.20.55. at 2.15 am.	
		1.30am	Patrol. Lt. Cooper and 12 O.R. left our lines PROWSE FARM. Object. Reconnoitre MILLCOTT and CRUMPFARM. To find out any hostile posts in vicinity and obtain information of hostile. Result: MILL COTT and adjoining dug-outs were thoroughly reconnoitred and contained no enemy. Dug-outs at E.6.a.4.7 and in vicinity of CRUMP FM were examined & found unoccupied. No hostile patrols were encountered & no signs of enemy movement seen. Many Very lights went up from WARWICK FM. Enemy seemed to be rather nervous. Five [?] of our own rifles were picked up on CAMBRIDGE Rd. at L.5.a.4.0.62. It was afterwards ascertained that these belonged to A¹ Div.	

Strength of Battalion. 31/5/18. Ration Strength. 27 Officers 749 O.R.

J.C. Steward Lt Col

I/R. Inniskilling Fus

Confidential

War Diary

of

1st Battalion The Royal Inniskilling Fus⁰

From: 1st June 1918.   To: 30th June 1918.

Army Form C. 2118.

WAR DIARY
or
INTELLIGENCE SUMMARY.
(Erase heading not required.)

1st R. Innis Fus.

Volume 39

Place	Date	Hour	Summary of Events and Information	Remarks and references to Appendices
FRONTLINE	1/6/18	11.30pm	Patrol 2 Lt J.S. Forsve and 12 O.R. left our lines PROWSE FM. **Object**: To confirm presence or otherwise of working party reported by O.P. at I.5.a. 40.85 during last evening. To lay in wait between CRUMP FM. and CAM BRIDGE Rd. to Western identification and confirm reports of progress as to possible attack. **Result**: No working party found or signs of any, no movement observed between CRUMP FM. and CAM BRIDGE Rd from I.5.a.5.5 very lights were sent up from trench commanded by E. of CRUMP FM. ROUTE PROWSE FM. and patrol going forward about 200x these dried to NEW COTT and I.5.a.5.5. returning through our listening post at I.4.b.7.8.6 I.4.b.25.70 at 2am. Patrol 2/Lt H.J. Higgs and 12 O.R. left our lines at c.28.6.5.4 **Object**: To search pill box & shelters in c.29.a and to locate any loop hole in the old trench c.29.a. **Result**: Pill boxes and shelters in c.29.a and old trench from c.29.a.6.55 to c.29.a.95.15 were found to be unoccupied. No signs of any loop hole actually were observed except distant transport and shouting. Very lights appeared to be put up from JASPER FM. The old trench was in very poor condition and showed no signs of occupation. Patrol returned through our wire reliefs at c.28.b.7.7.4 c.28.b.95.0 at 2-40am. Enemy artillery active. Shelling YPRES. to north.	

Army Form C. 2118.

WAR DIARY
or
INTELLIGENCE SUMMARY.
(Erase heading not required.)

Place	Date	Hour	Summary of Events and Information	Remarks and references to Appendices
FRONTLINE	2/11/16	10.30PM	Patrol 2/1 E. Yorks. and 2/OR. PROUSE FM C26 D 50.30 Object: Operate East of CAMBRIDGE Rd. to locate any hostile posts and to gain identification. Result: CRUMP FM all unoccupied. Three shell holes East of your lines found. Wof old trench at I 5a 96.50. Wounded and stretcher bearers seen at NEDEKE Rd. and track was entered at I 5a 96.50. Wounded and stretcher bearers seen at NEDEKE Rd. V. The trench was almost obliterated by shell fire, and no posts were located. MG opened fire from C29c 73. and was firing in a S.E. direction. Very lights continually about 1yd from WARWICK FM. When Patrol were on CAMBRIDGE Rd. at about I5a 3.5. enemy fired on the road with light trench mortars from direction of STABLES, forcing the patrol to walk along Route C28/1 60.30 to light railway - NEW CUT - CRUMP FARM - I5a 95.70. Patrol returned C25 c 60.30 aff 2am.	
	3/11/16	10.45am	Patrol 2/1 R.&L. Bridges and 12 O.Rs. C29c 10.50. Object: To operate in C.29, c with a view to obtaining an identification at C.29, C.50, 60. Result: Theos were heard in Pill Box C.29 c 60.60 but no movement was observed. The enemy were very much on the alert and the movement of the patrol was anxiously observed. Very lights continually went up from C.29, C.50, 60 and C29 c 50.70 and a machine gun opened fire on the patrol from about C.29 c 80.50. It was impossible to get sufficiently close to the post to rush it. Enemy artillery were a number of shells fell in our lines at C.26 & 6.2. and C28 D40.80, causing 4 killed 9 wounded.	

WAR DIARY or INTELLIGENCE SUMMARY

Army Form C. 2118.

Place	Date	Hour	Summary of Events and Information	Remarks and references to Appendices
V/LINE	3/6/18	10.30	Patrol. 2/Lt. Hamilton and 12 O.Rs. Prouse FM.C.26A4.0.2.0. **Object** To reconnoitre CAMBRIDGE Rd. as far as 25 a 4.5 and examine ground in vicinity for signs of enemy work. **Results** Patrol proceeded east of CAMBRIDGE Rd. 6.15 a 4.5. No signs of enemy were observed. Very lights were fired from about I.30 & 3' falls at MILL COT and NEW COT were examined and found to be unoccupied. No new work was found. **Route.** Along light railway from front of exit 6 mill Cot. Thence across YPRES – ZONNEBEKE Rd. Re L CAM BRIDGE Rd. Patrol returned C.28d.40.20 at 1.15 AM. Our and hostile artillery were active. Visibility was good no movement observed.	
	4/6/18		Small stationary patrols were sent out from the front line. The Lewis was relieved by the 3rd Battalion Grenadier Guards and two Belgium companies Guides on the night of 4th/5th-3/4/18. We entrained at Nor Bridge to proceed to TUNNELLERS CAMP. Sheet 27/F27A.	Vide Pon Order N.94
TUNNELLERS CAMP	5th 6th 7th 8th		The Battalion rests and cleans up. Training and smartening up under Company Commanders into Company football. The Battalion proceeds to Musketry Training Areas. Phases 2&3. The Battalion marched on 95. out of camp at 7AM. A and B Companies and Hd.Qr. (sig.) Coy Scouts and Snipers march to CASSEL AREA, & C and D Coys Scouts and Snipers entrained at ST. JANSTER BEZEN for	Vide Bn Order N.95

Army Form C. 2118.

WAR DIARY
or
INTELLIGENCE SUMMARY.
(Erase heading not required.)

Instructions regarding War Diaries and Intelligence Summaries are contained in F. S. Regs., Part II. and the Staff Manual respectively. Title pages will be prepared in manuscript.

Place	Date	Hour	Summary of Events and Information	Remarks and references to Appendices
CASSEL & RUBROUCK AREAS.	8th		A and B Coys and Battalion H.Q. less Scouts and Snipers in camp. Shut 27 P & 33 C and D Coys and Scouts and Snipers under Major Birmingham in billets. Shut 27 Coy. H7624 Coy. H7621. Coy. H7622. Coy. H7621. Bond B march into camp at midday. C and D Coy out at 12.30 P.M. Musketry unding with inter action competitions	
	9th-11th			
	12th		The Battalion returned to TUNNELLERS CAMP. C and D entrain at ST JANS TER BEZEN and arrive in camp at 2.30 P.M. A and B Coys march off at 4 P.M. and arrive in camp 8.30 P.M. Companies under Company Commanders.	Vide 169th Bn Defence Scheme Bn Order 96
	13th		The Battalion marches off at 8.30 A.M. for musketry training on PROVEN AERODROME ground.	
	14th		A and B companies train on PROVEN AERODROME. Instructors of 1st Bn and 9th Bn The Royal Irish Rifles Lectures by the Divisional Commander Maj Gen Hon Ya CBO. Presentation of medals to the following officers and men of the Battalion Bar to Military Cross. Lieut and Adjt Maj JC de Lacey D.M.C. Military Cross Capt T.W. May. Distinguished Conduct Medal. 15 TM B MacCormick. Military Medal 4257 Q.M.S. N Kemp. 15392 Sgt A Campbell 16337 Sgt R Murray 29144 Sgt J Pollock 10280 Sgt T Bedford 20442 Pte D Duggan. 31167 Pte W McGuinness. The Military Cross was awarded at the same time to Lt Pollock 2 Lt Crutten.	
	15th			
	16th			

Army Form C. 2118.

WAR DIARY
or
INTELLIGENCE SUMMARY.
(Erase heading not required.)

Place	Date	Hour	Summary of Events and Information	Remarks and references to Appendices
TUNNELLERS CAMP.	17		Battalion entrained after 12:30 am on PROVEN AERODROME 1 am. Companies under Company Commanders 4 pm. Marched to Camp. Sports held on the football field. Prizes presented by Brig Gen Heavy DSO. Companies at the disposal of Company Commanders. Recognisation of Platoons under the Battalion.	W.O.
	18			
	19-20		3rd section System carried out	Vide Pro. Orders 97.
PEKIN CAMP.	21		Battalion moved to PROVEN AREA. PEKIN CAMP. A.B. and D. Companies entrained at PUGWASH for WESTON HOEK at 4 am. C Company entrained PUGWASH 4.30 am for WESTON HOEK. Companies working. Strength 128 men work on EAST POPERINGHE line. Company at A 27 B 50. 1 Company at A 28 C 24. Company G 36.98.	
	22		Btlds. march off at 10.10 am via PROVEN to PEKIN CAMP. Companies find the same working parties. Football match against 6th Belgian Regiment. Won 4-1. The work: Companies find working parties of 100 men each for E POPERINGHE line. 90 men at work on gun pits under CRA.	
	23 24			
	25 26 27 28		Companies find working parties of 100 men each for work on E POPERINGHE line. The same working parties on E POPERINGHE line also 100 other ranks working on gun pits under CRA.	

Place	Date	Hour	Summary of Events and Information	Remarks and references to Appendices
	29th		Working Parties of 100 men per company on E POPERING HE Line.	
	30th		The Battalion moves to ROOSENDAAL Area. Companies find working parties of 100 men each for work on E POPERINGHE line. On completion of work parties march to Camp Vide Bn Order No. 95.	
			H.Q. Or Coy and details march off at 10.10 AM. Return Strength Offrs 32 Men 801	

Frederick ??? Lt Col
R Lewis Building ???

Confidential

War Diary

of

1st Battalion The Royal Inniskilling Fusiliers

From: 1st July 1918.   To: 31st July 1918.

Army Form C. 2118.

WAR DIARY
or
INTELLIGENCE SUMMARY.
(Erase heading not required.)

1st Royal Inniskilling Fusiliers

VOLUME 40

Instructions regarding War Diaries and Intelligence Summaries are contained in F. S. Regs., Part II. and the Staff Manual respectively. Title pages will be prepared in manuscript.

Places	Date	Hour	Summary of Events and Information	Remarks and references to Appendices
ROSSENDAAL AREA	July 1st		Holiday. Companies under Coy. commanders.	Vide Bn Order No. 99
	2nd		The Battalion move into area of the Reserve XVI French Corps. March from ROSSENDAAL to OXYCLAERE	Bn Order No. 100
OXYCLAERE	3rd		March to ZUYPEENE	
ZUYTPEENE	4th			
	5th		C.O. told Off. 1 officer per company and all platoon Sergts. go forward to reconnoitre Reserve position in the MONT DES CATS.	
	6th		Inspection of Companies by their Commanding Officer.	
MONT DES CATS	7th		Battalion marches to MONT DES CATS. March off 2.45 PM. Dispositions. Bn HqGrs & Vide Bn Order	Vide Bn Order 101
			R20a 85.40 A Coy. R14c13 B Coy. R26d 46.0 C Coy. R20c D Coy. R14d. Batt'n in billets by 2pm.	
	8th–11th		Cleaning up billets and training.	
	12th–13th		C Company move to R14c1.7.	Detour vide
	12th–13th		Companies at work breaking down crops in front of Support line R32c22 to R26d 86.	2nd Bn Order
	13th–14th		B Company move to R14c 6.9. Companies at work cutting down corn crops and cutting hay sown in front of the German line.	
	14th–16th		Companies at work digging a line in front of MT NOIR. M2Lq6 to M2d69.	

Army Form C. 2118.

WAR DIARY
or
INTELLIGENCE SUMMARY.
(Erase heading not required.)

Instructions regarding War Diaries and Intelligence Summaries are contained in F. S. Regs., Part II. and the Staff Manual respectively. Title pages will be prepared in manuscript.

Place	Date July	Hour	Summary of Events and Information	Remarks and references to Appendices
MT DE CATS	14th		All companies start work on the BLUE LINE on the forward edge of MT NOIR. Companies taken:- M26 to M26 & 7. divided between A.B.C. and D. Companies. Working parties marched off 9PM and cease work 2AM.	Ref/Sheet 28 SE.
	15-16		Work on MT NOIR continued.	
	17-18		Work ceases at 12 midnight and troops return to billets on account of expected Bosch attack. All grid coats haversack and supplies kept sent to transport lines for emergency. Battalion comft. at MAISON BLANCHE	
	19-20 20 21		Work continued all company tasks finished on this night. Recce party left at 3PM for MAISON BLANCHE. All 10% majors + fighter and tour in the [illegible] Coy left. Companies again at work on a new belt of wire in front of BLUE LINE. Prisoner bomb dropped on party. None killed 10 evacuated.	WD Batt order
	22nd		Coys on the wire in front of above line comfted and marked at the following Maces. R22 a 3.0 (29Ah) R32 b 5 (2Gph) R26 d 9.2 29Ah. R27d 5.3. R27 A95 R26 a 6.7 R26 d 8.2 (29Ah).	
	23/24		The Battalion moves to MT NOIR and becomes Support Battalion of Brigade in line. [illegible]	[illegible] 102.

WAR DIARY or INTELLIGENCE SUMMARY

Army Form C. 2118.

(Erase heading not required.)

Place	Date	Hour	Summary of Events and Information	Remarks and references to Appendices
PIT N11R	26-27		Companies at work as previous. Fine weather. No work under RE owing to shortage of material. 1 Platoon employed cutting gaps in wire of the Rlw line on Brigade front. 3 gaps in 200 yards of wire then 200 yards uncut 3 gaps in next 200 yards. Small leading party of Sman working for RE nightly.	Reformation
	27/28		1st Bn the Royal Inniskilling Fusiliers relieves 2nd Bn the Royal Inniskilling Fusiliers Vide Bn Order 103 in the line on the left sub sector of Left Brigade front, for disposition Vide attached map. At 11:30 PM while relief is in progress the Division on the left do a raid and the Bosch puts down a barrage on our front. A Company have 1 man killed 3 wounded. B Company have 1 killed and C Company 2 wounded. Relief complete by 2 AM. Band D Companies send out reconnoitring patrols of officer 60 R. The Acy Suppld Bosch officer to be very slack in this sector. The country in the moonlight	Vide Disposition Map Bn Right Bn Left Front Line Bn left Front Line The Acy Supld Reserve

WAR DIARY
or
INTELLIGENCE SUMMARY.
(Erase heading not required.)

Army Form C. 2118.

Place	Date	Hour	Summary of Events and Information	Remarks and references to Appendices
			of the trenches is practically undamaged all wire and deep standing. The front line is continuous but an art in places. Enemy machine guns active firing down valley in M.23.C. and d.	
	28/24.		Slightly increased artillery activity during the day. 7.45am to 3pm M.33.a and b shelled with 105 and 150 mm. About 200 shells in all. Hence at M.33.a 5.9 hit and set on fire exploding a dump of S.A.A. and bombs.	
	29/30		Artillery and machine gun activity normal. A Patrol of 21st Bedn and 70R left our lines on the night company front. They encountered 15 the enemy in the crops S/ TRESCAULT house and stood up and started of the enemy round them. They made a rush to get clear and two of the bombing them. They made a rush to get clear and two of the enemy gave way and they got through before returning, our own they turned and threw bombs at the enemy. 2 Lt Bredayon and 2 O.R. were slightly wounded.	

Army Form C. 2118.

WAR DIARY
or
INTELLIGENCE SUMMARY.
(Erase heading not required.)

Instructions regarding War Diaries and Intelligence Summaries are contained in F. S. Regs., Part II. and the Staff Manual respectively. Title pages will be prepared in manuscript.

Place	Date	Hour	Summary of Events and Information	Remarks and references to Appendices
	20/31		During the day 2 reconnaissance patrols situation 1OR and 2OR left our left company front and entered the house at She 50.50. It showed no signs of occupation. One of these patrols entered French at She 80.50 and found it unoccupied. At 10 PM 2Lt Newton and 7OR went out to house at She 50.50 as a machine gun had appeared to be firing from there but no signs of the enemy were seen. The Patrol began wait for there but no signs of the enemy were seen. Would artillery activity during the day. Artillery and machine guns very quiet at night until 2AM when artillery activity increased and the enemy put down a barrage on the Support company and near approaches. During the night the enemy appeared to be further away than previously.	

D. D. & L., London, E.C.
(A8094) Wt. W1771/M231 750,000 5/17 Sch. 52—Forms/C2118/14

WAR DIARY
or
INTELLIGENCE SUMMARY.

(Erase heading not required.)

Army Form C. 2118.

Place	Date	Hour	Summary of Events and Information	Remarks and references to Appendices
	31-1		Lt Welden visited sd6674 to Sd 30.95 with 6 OR and found it unoccupied. He went out again later with 11 OR and again reconnoitred this trench. Boche blankets were hanging on the dugout doors and a Boche rifle was found inside. The Blt of wire was found between this trench and the road. Hostile artillery was quiet during the day. A company relieves B Coy on right, company front. D company gone in to Support position. Relief of A Coy by C Coy postponed for 26 hours on account of rations coming up late.	V.D. Bn Order.

Robert Welden.
Commanding, 1st Batn The Royal Inniskillen Fusiliers

Confidential   X 39

Vol 31

War Diary

of

1st Battalion Royal Inniskilling Fusiliers

From 1st August. 1918.   To: 31st August. 1918.

Folio :-

WAR DIARY
INTELLIGENCE SUMMARY. 1ST BATTN THE ROYAL INNISKILLING F...

Place	Date	Hour	Summary of Events and Information	Remarks and references to Appendices
FRONT LINE LEFT SUBSECTOR ST JANS CAPPEL	August 1/2		Our Artillery Active. Enemy quiet. A Daylight patrol from the right company saw bev 7 Boches come out of the house at S3d 90.45 and proceed along the road through S3d towards BAILLEUL. A Lewis gun fire was opened on them and they disappeared at about 6 P.M. when reinforcements making a personal reconnaissance in Mo Mans Land Lieut Hughes surprised a Bosch near house at S4c 62.55 and made him surrender. Three others who were in the house were also captured and all four brought in. A Patrol of 1 officer 6 OR off right company front at 1.15 AM to reconnoitre house at S4d 91/95 when Bosh had been seen in the morning. Some Very lights were fired from it and machine gun opened fire. Transport washered on road from BAILLEUL to S3c 7.2 about 10.15 P.M. Our Artillery Active. Enemy Artillery Moderately Adn. Three patrols out in front of	W/s Divisional map
	2/3		our lines during the night. One patrol reconnoitred hedge from S4c 75 to S4c 60.55 and house at S4c 5.5. No trace of the enemy was seen. Another patrol left our lines at S4c69 and located an enemy post at S4c 9.7. Patrol from the right company heard the enemy talking in trench from S3c6.2 to S3c9.5. Enemy artillery activity increased during the day and shelled our S.Ps	
	3/4			

Army Form C. 2118.

WAR DIARY
or
INTELLIGENCE SUMMARY.
(Erase heading not required.)

Instructions regarding War Diaries and Intelligence Summaries are contained in F. S. Regs., Part II. and the Staff Manual respectively. Title pages will be prepared in manuscript.

Place	Date	Hour	Summary of Events and Information	Remarks and references to Appendices
MT NOIR.	4/5.		A heavy barrage from 9.30 pm to 10.30 pm and 11pm to 12 midnight. Enemy Aircraft showed increased Activity during the day, a reconnoitring machine flew very low over our lines at 8.30 pm. 1 patrol from this night (company visited house at S4c 55.85 at 12.30 AM. It was not occupied by the enemy who were in the trench to the East of it. Enemy artillery quiet except for a short strafe about 9pm.	
	5/6.		The Battalion is relieved by the 9th Battn the R.Inniskilling Fusiliers and proceeded to MT NOIR and became Reserve Battalion of the Brigade in the front line. Relief complete 11.50 p.m. Companies at work drawing shelters and making them waterproof, 1 Platoon at work on CT at M 32 L and 1 Platoon in M 36 a under the R.E. Work discontinued on account of very wet night. A+B and HQrs go to Baths at LAMANCHE.	Vide Battn Order No 103
	6/7.		1 Platoon at work on CT in M32L under RE. 1 Platoon wiring in front of front line in Lt Battn Sector. Watch on water carriers and Refreshments to Baths at LAMANCHE.	

WAR DIARY or INTELLIGENCE SUMMARY

Army Form C. 2118.

Place	Date	Hour	Summary of Events and Information	Remarks and references to Appendices
	7/8.		2 Platoons working on CT on M12.6 and M33a under the R.E. 1 Platoon working on repairing road at R30a5.3 to M31.6.0. 1 Officer wounded 2 men killed on A Company quarry when forming up for working party. 2Lt BUMSTEAD.	Vide Batt Order No 104
MONT DES CATS	8/4.		The Battalion is relieved by the 1st Battn The Royal Irish Fusiliers and proceeds to BRIDEFM Area MONT DES CATS. The 109th Brigade becomes Reserve Brigade of the 36th Division.	
	9th 10th		Cleaning up. Working party from B Company at work on BLUE LINE M35t. Divisional Band. Training: D Coy at work on light Railway in R36. This work continued till 14th.	
	11th, 12th		Church Parade with Divisional Band. A and C Companies at work deepening and duck boarding BLUE LINE R55t. 6.6 to R36 a 9.7. Coys making up knife rests. Lt J Duff. Lt H.G. Stewart 2Lt Washington & Lt Mahony join the Battalion.	
	12.13		B and C Companies at work on BLUE LINE in R35t and R36a. Also inspected by CO in B Company at work deepening CT on Right Battn Sector S2985. B Company at	
	13th-14th		work wiring on SCHAEXKEN - ST JANS CAPPEL road. Heavy gas shelling of forward areas specially ST JANS CAPPEL valley. B Company watering party returned till night to fill up but were affected by the gas (Mustard) at 8 AM next morning. 2 Officers & OR becoming 10R wounded. 2Lt HENDERSON and 2Lt MACARTHY. Co inspected by CO in 114.	

Army Form C. 2118.

WAR DIARY
or
INTELLIGENCE SUMMARY.
(Erase heading not required.)

Place	Date	Hour	Summary of Events and Information	Remarks and references to Appendices
	14-15		D Coy and 2 Platoons of C Coy at work on CT in Right Battn Sector widening and deepening. S28 80.50 to S28 90.20.	
	15-16		2 Platoon A Coy work on Drams on Potijie to M31 b.77. C Coy at work widening and duckboarding R 35 b.	
	16-17		D Coy and 2 Platoons A Coy working on night CT., 2 Platoons C Coy duckboarding BLUE Line in R 35 a. A Coy at work on CT on M 32 a and b.	
	17-18		Company drawing. No work in g portion at night.	
	18-19		A Coy and 2 Platoons of C Coy at work on Lt Battn CT M 26 d 70.	
	19th 19-20		Details who formed 18% during last tour in the trenches join the Battalion. 2 Platoons A Coy at work on Decauville Track for mon dugouts M 31 6.8.6. 2 Platoons B Coy working in front of BLUE LINE M 31 6.7b to M 31 6 9.9. B Coy at work on CT in right Brigade Sector. A Coy on CT Right Brigade Sector.	
	20-21		A and B Coy at work on night CT S 28 8.3.	
	21-22		HQ Coy at work on Decauville Track M 31 688. C and D working on right CT widening and deepening, S 28 84.	
	22-23		H Coy and C and D working on BLUE LINE M 31 b 5.9. A and B Companies at work on	

Army Form C. 2118.

WAR DIARY
or
INTELLIGENCE SUMMARY.
(Erase heading not required.)

Place	Date	Hour	Summary of Events and Information	Remarks and references to Appendices
	23-24		Right CT on 52 a 77. At 11:30 PM Bosch attack deliver a counter attack on the right Brigade front and put down a Heavy Barrage on CT when party was working. A Company casualties 2/Lt WASHINGTON MC killed. Lt IRVINE wounded. 3 OR killed. 20 OR wounded. 14 OR gassed. B Coy. 10 R killed 3 OR wounded. Advanced parties of Officer party and 1 NCO per Platoon go forward to spend night in the line with 1st Batt. The Royal Irish Fusiliers (Coy in support) 1 Platoon on Dicconail(Troops M.S. 16 88. 2 Platoons a 2 Platoons D Coy on CT Right Brigade Sub-Sector.	Vide Batt Order No 102. Vide Original Map.
FRONT LINE	24-25		The Battalion relieves 1st Batt. The Royal Irish Fusiliers in Front Line Left Battalion Sector. Left Brigade Sub Sector. Dispositions: Right Front Line B Coy. Left Front Line D Coy. Support A Coy. Reserve C Coy. Relief complete 1:30 a.m. Casualties during relief 1 officer killed Lt J Duff At 4:30 AM the enemy put down a barrage of LTMs on our post at S.S.D 94 and attacked it with about 20 men. They were beat off by rifle and L.G fire. Our casualties 1 killed 8 wounded. Another attack on this post was attempted at 6:30 A.M. When 5 men were seen within 5 yards. They were disposed by	

Army Form C. 2118.

WAR DIARY
or
INTELLIGENCE SUMMARY.
(Erase heading not required.)

Instructions regarding War Diaries and Intelligence Summaries are contained in F. S. Regs., Part II. and the Staff Manual respectively. Title pages will be prepared in manuscript.

Place	Date	Hour	Summary of Events and Information	Remarks and references to Appendices
			rifle and L.G fire.	
	25-26		Enemy artillery quiet. Was put out S3d 85 to S3c 83	
	26-27.		Post in Bosch Farm at S3d 90.35 withdrawn without interruption by the enemy. Withdrawal covered by patrol of 1 officer 4 O.R. At 11 P.M. a Bosch patrol at S3e 50.52 was dispersed by fire from our post. A patrol from night company went down ridge from S3d 5.4 towards HAEGEDOORNE when an M.G. was located. Patrol then moved across company front to TOMLIN P.M. Platoon in TOMLIN'S Fm. Patrolled. Prisoners cage in front of River hut. Patrol from left company arrested from right House at S3d 90.44 and S4c 62.12 no sign of enemy was seen.	
	27-28.		Enemy Artillery quiet during the day, more active at night. Two patrols were cut in front of our lines at night. 1 Sgt 6 men went out at S4c B.K. towards trench at S4e 90.70. Patrol came under fire on reaching enemy wire and had to withdraw. 1 Officer 12 O.R. left S3c 90.45 at 10 P.M. and proceeded towards HAEGEDOORNE they did not come in contact with the enemy. At about 4.30 P.M. a large dump was exploded behind enemy lines and numerous fires were observed in his back areas. During the night trench was dug dug from S3d 5.5 to S3d 95.20. Houses at S3d 90.44	

WAR DIARY or INTELLIGENCE SUMMARY

Army Form C. 2118.

Place	Date	Hour	Summary of Events and Information	Remarks and references to Appendices
	16.29		A man who attempted to approach post at Sqd 55.46 with Bomb was shot. He belonged to Norley half Battn 118 TR. Patrol from Left Comp. visited house at Sqc 52.46 and found it unoccupied. Trench dug from S3.05.20 to Sqc 70.90. Enemy Artillery very quiet but this MG's active. No Man's Land and approaches to the line. Numerous Very lights. Enemy sun american.	
	29.30		to make their presence felt. A very large number of fires lighted within enemy's line at dusk. Two large explosions occurred about 3 a.m. Our front patrolled continuously during the night but saw no indications of enemy's forward posts having been withdrawn. At 10.30 a.m. (30th) a patrol of B Coy entered the Beach Line and dispersed a post of 8 men at S4c.6.5 bringing back 1 prisoner who afterwards gave valuable information about the intentions of the enemy. A Coy patrol of D Coy pushed out to Sqc 2.15 with out encountering any enemy on observing the retreat of this patrol D Coy advanced in conjunction with the 2nd Royal Inniskillen 5 Fusiliers at 11 a.m. taking up the line Sqc 5.7 to S10a.9.4. D Coy moved of at 11.30 p.m. and took	

WAR DIARY
or
INTELLIGENCE SUMMARY.
(Erase heading not required.)

Army Form C. 2118.

Instructions regarding War Diaries and Intelligence Summaries are contained in F.S. Regs., Part II. and the Staff Manual respectively. Title pages will be prepared in manuscript.

Place	Date	Hour	Summary of Events and Information	Remarks and references to Appendices
	31st		up the line S10a 9.3 to S1d 5.2 both moving their rear flank to cover their left flank. Battalion H.Q. was established at S3d 5.8 at 11.30 p.m. At 4 p.m. the whole line moved forward to the road WINSTON ROW – VASSAL F.M. SH 6.9.5 which then was held for the night. At 5.15 a.m. orders were issued for a general advance to take place at 6 a.m. At 5.30 a.m. V.d. Bde One O.C. Bomb D'cap working on their own indication of advantages of advancing thick. mist pushed forward strong patrols and by 6 a.m. RAVELSBERG was in our hands. At 6 a.m. Bomb and D Companies moved forward across the hill and took up a position along THORNTON ROAD S23a 0.4 to S17 d 8.2. Considerable resistance on the hill was encountered during this advance after crossing RAVELSBERG Road (it was successfully overcome by the combined fire of our Lewis guns. Battalion Head quarters moved forward to S17 a 4.3 from which point visual communication with Bde HQ at TRISCOTT H.O S3d 2.7 was successfully maintained. A Company moved up to S17 a 6.3 and C Company to S1dd <s>6.8.3/7</s> 5.5. After reaching THORNTON ROAD in compliance with Brigade Orders O.C 12nd Royal Inniskillings	4 I.

WAR DIARY
or
INTELLIGENCE SUMMARY.
(Erase heading not required.)

Army Form C. 2118.

Place	Date	Hour	Summary of Events and Information	Remarks and references to Appendices
			Battalion moved by to form and advanced guard to cover the 109th Brigade front with 2nd R Innisskillings Battalion in support and 9th R Innisskilling Fusiliers in Reserve. The Battalion front then extended from S23c 0.4 to S18c 2.3 with Bomb Companies in front. On R Innisskilling Fusiliers received orders to change the direction. At the front OC 10th R Innisskilling Fusiliers received orders to change the direction of the advance so as to conform with the Boundaries. Right S23c0.4 S20d1.4 then main Road to ARMENTIERES. Left Boundary. S16c23 to S19b55. This brought the Right flank to S23d27 (approx) S18c 2.3 his advance was then continued at 11.40 am to front line companies with his Right flank to S20d8.9 and Left to S17d8.9 S18c 2.3 in position from S29b66 to S18c 5.2 with patrols in GOUGH HOUSE at this point the troops on the right and left were held up which necessitated a halt on this line. Enemy M/G very active and his field guns shelled our advanced companies. This position was maintained during the night.	Percival Col.
T/Lt Col. Comm. ?

Confidential

War Diary
—of—
1st Royal Inniskilling Fusiliers,

From 1st Sept 1918   To 30th Sept 1918

WAR DIARY 1ST BATTN THE ROYAL INNISKILLING FUSILIERS
INTELLIGENCE SUMMARY
VOLUME 42

Army Form C. 2118.

Place	Date SEPT	Hour	Summary of Events and Information	Remarks and references to Appendices
	1		At dawn the 9th Battn the Royal Inniskilling Fusiliers sent out strong patrols through the line of the 1st Battalion and the advance was continued by the 2nd and 9th Battalions the Royal Inniskilling Fusiliers, the 1st Battalion becoming Battalion in Support to the 109th Brigade. Their advance was delayed till 2 p.m. after which the 2nd Battn on the left advanced to the Western outskirts of NEUVE EGLISE, D Coy of the 1st Battn moving up in Support. After dark that night the 108th Brigade relieved the 109th Brigade and the Battalion moved back into billets in the vicinity of WOLF HOEK. The casualties during the 3 days operations were as follows :- Other Ranks 10 killed 24 wounded	Vide Bm Order 106 Vide 109 Bd Order
	2nd 3rd		The Battalion in billets in WOLFHOEK area	Vide 109 Bd Order No 19
	4th		Orders received to move up to RACLE FM RAVELSBERG Battalion in billets by 9 pm. Commanding Officer conveyed a congratulations of the Corps Commander on the way in which the Battalion got into Rosch line when they had previously withdrawn his outposts on the way the three days operations in following him up were carried out	Vide Bn Order 107
	5th		The Battalion moved forward to relieve the 109th Brigade 1st R Irish Rifles in the Support Brigade area then at 7:30 pm. Heavy gas shelling of the area from 12:30 AM to 4 AM	Vide Bd Order

Army Form C. 2118.

WAR DIARY
or
INTELLIGENCE SUMMARY.
(Erase heading not required.)

Instructions regarding War Diaries and Intelligence Summaries are contained in F.S. Regs., Part II. and the Staff Manual respectively. Title pages will be prepared in manuscript.

Place	Date SEPT	Hour	Summary of Events and Information	Remarks and references to Appendices
	6-8		4000 shells reported to have fallen in support Brigad. Area. Casualties in the Battalion 2 officers wounded Capt. 2 Lt HUGHES. 2 LT NEWTON OR 6 wounded 900 company killed wounded. On the 7th GHQ 2nd line East of NEUVE EGLISE recommisited by all officers and Platoon Sergts.	
	8		The Battalion move back to RAEGE FM area. March off 4 P.M. Companies disposed as follows. Bm HQ S16b.1.6 A Coy S16b1.6 B Coy S16c.5.6 B Coy S16c.1.5 A Coy S16c.9.7 C Coy S16c1.5 D Coy S16c 75.70	
	9		Company training. 1 Platoon per company sent to take all ammunition left in the old line occupied by the battalion before the advance of Sept 30th. New huts built to accommodate the battalion.	
	10-13th			
	15.		On the night of 15/16 the battalion proceeds to support Mongolia area and relieve the 2nd Royal Irish Rifles dispositions. Bm HQ T10b.7.9. A Coy T17 & S 1.6 B Coy T11d.01 C Coy T11o.7.5 D Coy T10 d 1.7	Vide Bm Orders 108
	16		On the night 16/17 B Coy were the frontline on the 109 Bde front. D Company supplying {company HQrs} Winers of the front continued by C Coy company chantier line found from A Coy.	
	17		The Battalion is relieved by the 15th Bn London Rifles relief complete 11.30 pm. Battalion proceeds to the Teen shot LINUSAPELLEOL for the night.	B.O. 109.
	19			
	20		The Battalion marches of GODEWAERSVELD march off 8pm arrive 10.30 p.m.	Vide Bm Order 110.
	21		Rest and general cleaning up. Drafts rejoin the Battalion.	

WAR DIARY
or
INTELLIGENCE SUMMARY.
(Erase heading not required.)

Army Form C. 2118.

Place	Date	Hour	Summary of Events and Information	Remarks and references to Appendices
	22nd		Battalion marched to WORMHOUDT.	
	23-25		Company training.	
	26.		Orders received to move to SCHOOL CAMP. The battalion marched off at 7.35pm and moving via HERZEELE - HOUTKERQUE and N of WATOU arrived at School SCHOOL CAMP 11.45pm.	Vide Bn Order No III
	27		The Battalion marched out of SCHOOL CAMP at 8 PM and arrived DIRTY BUCKET CAMP at 10 PM.	Vide Bn Order No 112
	28		The Battalion entrains at HAGEL Station in the afternoon and proceeds by train to the Northern outskirts of YPRES thence after a short halt by road to I.II.b.2.5 arriving at 8.30 pm and remaining for the night.	Vide Bn Order 113.
	29th		At 5.30 AM Orders are received for a further advance and after a short halt at WEST HOEK and in the vicinity of J.7.d.9. arrives at REUTEL, ahalt after noon when it halts pending further orders. At 3 PM intimation was received that a gap in the front line existed between	

WAR DIARY
or
INTELLIGENCE SUMMARY

Army Form C. 2118.

Place	Date	Hour	Summary of Events and Information	Remarks and references to Appendices
			The right of the 2nd R Inniskillings involved and the left of the 29th Division and the battalion was ordered to fill it. The OC 1st R Inn: Inniskillings Fusiliers moved his battalion forward and placing his left on the MOLENHOEK - TERHAND road so as to maintain touch with the battalion on that flank decided to occupy the high ground running through K15b4 K21b. and in the hope of linking up with the 29th Division on the right no indication whatever of the likely whereabouts of that Division was available At this period only half an hour daylight remained which added to the existing difficulties. The Battalion with two companies in the front line and two in support debouched from the neighbourhood of MOLENHOEK and moved forward on either side of KIT FARM. Enemy Machine Guns from the direction of TERHAND immediately opened fire and during the advance an enemy gun at very close range and probably firing with open sights caused casualties it being here that Lieut Hamilton fell. The battalion	

WAR DIARY
or
INTELLIGENCE SUMMARY.
(Erase heading not required.)

Army Form C. 2118.

Place	Date	Hour	Summary of Events and Information	Remarks and references to Appendices
			succeeded in reaching their objective shortly after dark and took up an outpost position for the night. They were in touch with the Battalion on the left although patrols worked unceasingly throughout the night no communication with the 29th Division could be effected. The work of these patrols however was made extremely difficult owing to the heavy rain which fell throughout the night the fit on darkness and the fact that no information as to the likely position of the 29th Division was available. The casualties during the half hour advance over the open in the evening were. 1 officer killed. Lieut HAMILTON. 2 O.Rs killed. 8 O.R wounded.	

F.C.Dent Lt Colonel
Commanding 1st Bn The Royal Inniskilling Fusiliers

Confidential

109/36

War Diary

-of-

1st Battalion, The Royal Inniskilling Fusiliers

From:- 1st October 1918   To:- 31st October 1918

Folio - 43.

Vol 313

WAR DIARY or INTELLIGENCE SUMMARY. 1ST BATT'N THE ROYAL INNISKILLING FUSILIERS

VOLUME 43

Army Form C. 2118.

Place	Date Oct	Hour	Summary of Events and Information	Remarks and references to Appendices
	1		At an early hour the 108th Brigade moved through our position to continue the attack. At in compliance with Brigade Orders the Battalion moved to the outskirts of DADIZEELE and then further were ordered to move forward to RICHMOND Cross Roads and taken the latter place as a point to swing round attacking from North to South, and eventually occupy the SONSHINE CORNER-MOUNTAIN road. In the face of small opposition this would have been an easy matter. On reaching RICHMOND Cross Roads the situation was found to be intense as there was no doubt an was forward afterwards that an enemy observation post in LEDEGHEM church observed the advance of the battalion from the time it left the outskirts of DADIZEELE. The Battalion swung round and executed a perfect advance along the RICHMOND cross roads MANHATTAN FM road. At 1430 orders were received from Brigade that the village of DADIZEELE HOEK should be taken. At this time the advance of the battalion was held up by rifle fire from several enemy strong points on the outskirts of TEOFANI CROSSING. In order to clear the situation TEOFANI CROSSING and neighbourhood had first to be cleared of the enemy. The OC 1st Royal Innisklg Fus'rs detailed attack the CROSSING and adjacent strong points with three companies in support line	

WAR DIARY or INTELLIGENCE SUMMARY

Army Form C. 2118.

Place	Date	Hour	Summary of Events and Information	Remarks and references to Appendices
			The attack on the left might have been successful with the necessary artillery preparation but this was not forthcoming. Immediately the attack was launched enemy Machine Guns opened fire from all directions. In spite of this opposition the battalion pushed forward until the casualties occurring specially to officers showed that a further attempt to advance would be foolhardy. Consequently as darkness was then setting in the line L16 c 4.3 L13 a 9.1 L13 a 9.5 L13 a 3.9 was taken up. Touch was maintained throughout with units on the right and left. The casualties in this afternoon were Officer 7 wounded ORs 17 killed, 97 wounded, 5 missing.	
	October 2nd		The day passed quietly and very little enemy movement was observed. At 16.00 the enemy commenced shelling our positions and the approaches to PADIZEELE. At 17.00 the bombardment had become intense and it was then apparent that an attack on the part of the enemy was intended. Shortly before 1800 an extremely heavy barrage fell on the ROULERS-MENIN road and extended in depth up to the outskirts of PADIZEELE. Immediately after the barrage the enemy attacked in force. The front of the attack coming against B Company	

which was then the right company on the line through weight of numbers our right was forced back till our Lewis Gun on the left ally afforded by two Machine Guns in Gheluvelt were repeatedly held back and by dint of tireless firemanship the enemy advance. This however enabled the OC B Coy to now games his company and bring up his own forward with a ringing chur drove back the enemy in disorder and on rallying pushed forward a distance of 200 yards beyond the original position. He was however caught in flank by enemy Machine Guns and decided to withdraw to the original line.

The casualties during the afternoon were particularly light considering the intensity of the enemy bombardment. ORs 12 killed 14 wounded.

The attay passed quietly though the enemy afterwards at 10h nervous as to but down a barrage on the outskirts of NADIZEELE and through burning woods at morning and evening stand to.

Both OC 1st Royal Innishilling Fusiliers had all four companies in the front line he decided to withdraw one platoon each from A and D companies to form a local support B company line now reduced to two platoons

October 3rd

Army Form C. 2118.

WAR DIARY
or
INTELLIGENCE SUMMARY.
(Erase heading not required.)

Instructions regarding War Diaries and Intelligence Summaries are contained in F. S. Regs., Part II. and the Staff Manual respectively. Title pages will be prepared in manuscript.

Place	Date	Hour	Summary of Events and Information	Remarks and references to Appendices
	4		This was another quiet day though there was some counter preparation on outskirts of NOIZEELE at various fend to Jn the vecinity the battalion is relieved by 12th Royal Irish Rifles and proceeds to support Area Kingd Vut Extn. The Total casualties during these operations were	October 11.

OFFICERS

KILLED

LIEUT HAMILTON W

WOUNDED

CAPT McLEAN J
2 LIEUT ARMSTRONG W A
2 LIEUT LEGG H G
2 LIEUT MAHONEY E A
2 LIEUT HODGSON W
2 LIEUT SOPER S J
2 LIEUT ASHMORE A S
LIEUT MILLER F E. MORC (Att)
LIEU WOUNDED

OTHER RANKS

KILLED
14

163

WAR DIARY
or
INTELLIGENCE SUMMARY.
(Erase heading not required.)

Army Form C. 2118.

Place	Date	Hour	Summary of Events and Information	Remarks and references to Appendices
	5-6		The Battalion was in rest and engaged in Inner-Outpost	V.C. 109 Patl Order No 54 M.L.
	7		The Battalion moved to DIRTY BUCKET CAMP. March discipline was in train at BROODSEINDE in light Railway 16.30. Arrived in camp 21.30	
	8		Cleaning up and amusement	
	9-10		Companies training under Company Commanders	
	10-11		Company training. Football match against 74th Regiment d'Infanterie	
	12		The Battalion moved forward by train from HAGEL Sin to BROODSEINDE thence by march Battn Ord 119 route to K7b, when it went into bivouac for the night.	Battn Ord 119
	13		The Battalion marched off at 10 pm for the front line and got into position preparatory for attack next day as follows :- A Company on the right C Company on the left in a new trench dug by the 15th Royal Rifles from K1946.9 to K1366.7 B Company on the right and D Company on the left took up their positions on our own front line immediately in rear of this trench. Battalion HQ followed the rear of the trench. Battalion Hd Qrs was situated at SAGO Farm K136.5.9. The Battalion was in position by 02.00. At 05.53 our barrage opened and Germans Barrage immediately fell on our front line causing a good many casualties.	W.M. Rd Order No 60 Battn Order 120 Vide Batt Appendix Battn Order 120
	14		At 05.35 all companies left their assembly trench and advanced under the Barrage.	MAP

WAR DIARY
or
INTELLIGENCE SUMMARY.
(Erase heading not required.)

Army Form C. 2118.

Place	Date	Hour	Summary of Events and Information	Remarks and references to Appendices
			the support companies gaining their distance as soon as clear of the hostile barrage. The resistance of the enemy was slight until DADIZEELE HOEK was reached, particularly from two pill boxes near DADIZEELE HOEK. It was during this first stage that 2 Lt IRVINE was killed. This resistance was quickly overcome by our determined attack and a large number of prisoners secured. From a hill east of MARCOUITCH crossing 3 officers and 30 ORs were mopped up after the front line had passed. After DADIZEELE HOEK the resistance of the enemy was not so stiff, but the thickness combined with the smoke of our barrage made it impossible to see more than 10 yards and made the keeping of direction very difficult and communication almost impossible. The ground over which the Battalion was attacking was marshy in places, both of which, and crossed by two streams the KLEINE BEEKE and HEULEBEEKE. "A" Company commander advanced by compass and at 06.00 had gained the line L17.C.4.0 to L.19.a.6.3. "D" Company came under heavy machine gun fire from the houses at L.17.d.9.	

WAR DIARY
or
INTELLIGENCE SUMMARY.

(Erase heading not required.)

Army Form C. 2118.

Place	Date	Hour	Summary of Events and Information	Remarks and references to Appendices
			Capt Maxshe had already been twice wounded immediately swung his company to the right charged the house with a cheer and cleared them of the enemy. He then occupied the farm at L17 c 8.5 securing possession of a battery of field guns. This position was caught with machine gun fire from the village of MOORSEELE but our Lewis gun returned the fire with such good effect that B company on the right was able to advance and the Brigade on the night was materially assisted in their attack on MOORSEELE which organisation this position Capt Mary was again wounded. B company 2nd Batt. R. Royal Inniskilling Fusiliers came up on the ☆ left and reinforced C company to the right of the 29th Divn at K17a9.5. From this position the line was advanced to the firm of the road K17d22 to K17 b 5.5 when the 2nd Batt. the Royal Inniskilling Fusiliers passed through toward GULLEGHER supported by the 9th Batt. the Royal Inniskilling Fusiliers and the battalion which was now in support were dug in with companies disposed as follows:-
B company on the right and D company on the left on line ⚹ ⚹ ⚹	

WAR DIARY
or
INTELLIGENCE SUMMARY.

Army Form C. 2118.

Place	Date	Hour	Summary of Events and Information	Remarks and references to Appendices
	Oct 16th		touch was established with the 15th Royal Irish Rifles at DOROTHY BRIDGE and with the 29th Division on the left. A Company was withdrawn to support at K.17.d.1.9 and C Company to remain at K.16.d.5.8. when Battalion Head Quarters was established. The Battalion remained here for the night. In this attack the Battalion gained its objectives in scheduled time and captured 11 field guns, the Enemy Companies on rear of these batteries in the fog had it fixed for eleven. They had present 11 O.O.R. E Company sent a party of men hurriedly dealt with the situation. The number of machine guns both heavy and light which was captured was estimated at 50. One TM was captured. All prisoners captured about 200.	Vide Bn Order AS.B.
		11.00	At 14.00 the 2nd Battn Royal Inniskilling Fusiliers attacked GALLIPOLI and the 1st Battn moved forward behind the 9th Battn. On reaching its line Gr. Peuton the 9th Battn passed through the 2nd Battn Royal Inniskilling Fusiliers and the HEURE FM in DUE moved up in support to Farm L 4.20 Heuters redeemed their position at 4.22 a 64. Headquarters established 4.22 a 64.	

WAR DIARY
INTELLIGENCE SUMMARY. THE ROYAL INNISKILLING FUSILIERS
1st BATTN.

Army Form C. 2118.

Place	Date	Hour	Summary of Events and Information	Remarks and references to Appendices
	Oct 15		Information was received from O.C. 9th Battn Royal Innniskilling Fusiliers that the battalion had captured HEULE and was in position in the railway to the East of it and in touch with the 29th on its left and the right flank was in the air. It was then discovered that the Brigade on the right was held up on the line of K.22.c.6.3. - K.22.c.6.3. O.C. 1st Battn The Royal Inniskilling Fusiliers ordered "B" & "D" Companies men to cover the flank. "D" Company to take up position along the line of the HEULEBEKE from K.22.b.5.4 to K.22.a.2.5. "B" Company line running due south along the GULLEGHEM - HEULE Road and astride the form at K.22 a.b.2 and twenty from the advance to these forms was carried out under heavy machine gun fire though no casualties occurred. While this movement was being carried out a message was received from the Brigade on the right that they were short of officers with artillery support. The Battalion no sooner in touch with the Brigade on the right moved forward at the same time as "B" Company and presently from	C.G C.G

Army Form C. 2118.

WAR DIARY
or
INTELLIGENCE SUMMARY.
(Erase heading not required.)

1st BATTN. THE ROYAL INNISKILLING FUSILIERS

Place	Date	Hour	Summary of Events and Information	Remarks and references to Appendices
	Oct 15		At 15h5 orders were received that the 2 9 th Brigade were about to advance on the left and that the 103rd Brigade would relieve the garrison of the LYS without the slightest movement, and that the 1st Battn Royal Inniskilling Fusiliers was to send forward their O conference at 15:00 to clear the triangle formed by the HEULEBEKE railway and the Menin divisional boundary in G 10 and H 13 keeping touch with 2nd Dnr and 103rd Brigade. The O.C. 1st Battn. The Royal Inniskilling Fusiliers immediately ordered "C" & "D" Companies forward to do this but at 16:30 a counter attack was received and three Companies were shifted and sent to their original position. As the situation on the right flank was now serious by the advance of the 2nd Inniskn Fusrs who were without "B" Company was unknown and these about G 17 & 92 m were unknown to the 9th Battn Royal Inniskn Fusiliers. Or 16:40 Headquarters were moved up to G 17 a.0.3 to be in close touch with the 9th Battalion. At 17:00 further orders were received that were previously ordered was to be carried by the 1st Battn The Royal Inniskilling Fusiliers.	109th Bde Orders MS6

WAR DIARY
INTELLIGENCE SUMMARY

1st Battn. THE ROYAL INNISKILLING FUS.

Army Form C. 2118.

Place	Date	Hour	Summary of Events and Information	Remarks and references to Appendices
	15.		"C" & "D" Companies were ordered forward to do this. The Company Commanders of these two Companies went forward to make a personal reconnaissance and got in touch with the 29th Division who were advancing on the left and with the 2nd Royal Irish Rifles on the right who had come up to their lines of its advancing. They then advanced with their companies and reached the line of the road, i.e. it was where that the 29th Division had reached the LYs at H.21.c.0.8. At 00 1st Battn the Royal Irish Rifles reported that LYs at H.25.d.3.5 were known up by the enemy and before the Battn reached the river. At about 23.60 orders were received that all troops must be withdrawn behind the railway by 05.00 a.m. The 109th Brigade were to cover the passage of the LYs. Communication was extremely difficult owing to the information that the Battalion had	

WAR DIARY
INTELLIGENCE SUMMARY

1st BATTN THE ROYAL INNISKILLING FUS

Army Form C. 2118.

Place	Date	Hour	Summary of Events and Information	Remarks and references to Appendices
	15		already return so far as the L.G's could not be sent to the Brigade in time to state this attack. "C" & "D" Companies had therefore to be withdrawn behind the railway which was held by the Royal Inniskilling Fusiliers. These three Companies were then billeted in villages in HEULE.	109th Bde DR1
	16th		At 14.00 orders were received that the Battalion should march at once to LEDEGHEM where they arrived at 17.00. They were into billets there for the first Qunium relieving the 36th. Casualties during these two days Operations were:- 2/Lieutenant B.W. Jannow Killed. 2/Lieut. T.W. May Wounded. Other Ranks Killed - 25. Other Ranks Wounded - 118.	109th Bde LD2

Major
Commanding 1st Bn. The Royal Inniskilling Fusiliers

Army Form C. 2118.

WAR DIARY
or
INTELLIGENCE SUMMARY.
(Erase heading not required.)

Instructions regarding War Diaries and Intelligence Summaries are contained in F. S. Regs., Part II. and the Staff Manual respectively. Title pages will be prepared in manuscript.

Place	Date	Hour	Summary of Events and Information	Remarks and references to Appendices
	13th		The Battalion rode in LEDEGHEM. Salvage parties from A Company were sent out to work over the ground captured on the attack operations of 14th–16th and also captured enemy material. They collected a large number of enemy machine guns, Lewis guns and rifles, and the clearance of the battalion area from gun magazines etc was completed by Saturday.	100th Bn Order 85 Batt. Order. 122
	16th		The 36th Division relieved the 2nd Belgian Division. The battalion moved forward by march route and went into billets in support in B19 and B23 (occupying B1 Central). The Battalion relieved by the 11th Regiment Belgian Infantry. As the situation on the eastern front of Blanc Bn Control to B & 25 was uncertain no platoon of Bn Company was placed at C7 & 89. During the night the LT5 was reconnoitred in Kiga Massage order was issued for the troops of the 4th, 5th, 6th and 9th Battalion. The Battalion marched forward.	100th Bn 69 MAP
	19th		Reynolds? Lt Colonel … … Battalion was not passed till 16.35 when the battalion moved forward. The Company Officers road through the Orders with the Company Commanders.	

WAR DIARY
or
INTELLIGENCE SUMMARY

Army Form C. 2118.

Sheet 2.

Place	Date	Hour	Summary of Events and Information	Remarks and references to Appendices
	10th October		Some neutral patrols "C" & "D" Companies were made responsible for the capture of SPRIETE and DESSELGHEM respectively. "A" and "B" Companies passing through "B" & "D" Companies for DRIES and SPRIETE. "A" and "B" Companies were responsible for the protection of the right flank through DRIES and SPRIETE. At 21:30 the Battalion moved off by Companies with an interval of 50 yards between Platoons down the track past C.15.d.5.3	0.B.18.6.3
		C.19.a.10 to B.19.a.11	where a bridge was constructed by the Royal Engineers which was completed just as the Battalion arrived there. The machine guns in the ridge and got into position from B.20.w.0.0 to B.20.1.5 though the shell fire on the west side of the river was considerable. The position was reached without casualties. The advance was established at B.19.d.9.9 at 23:00 and advanced Battalion H.Q. at B.1.w.3. From there was the Battalion again move forward & then forming up position D by from C.20.w.2.2, C.20.w.8.5. "B" Company C.20.w.8.5 to C.21.b.8.5 C. Coy "A" Company behind them In this position they came under very heavy Machine gun fire and a most determined counter attack was launched against "B" Company on the right. This attack was beaten off.	9.

WAR DIARY
INTELLIGENCE SUMMARY

Army Form C. 2118.

Sheet 3.

Place	Date	Hour	Summary of Events and Information	Remarks and references to Appendices
	18th October		with rifle, Lewis gun and machine gun fire and the following day at least 25 Germans dead were found lying in front of the farm at L.20.c.2.0. with several Machine Guns. During the counter attack Captain Woolley M.C. who was walking about encouraging his men was wounded. At 02.00 as soon as our barrage ceased the Battalion moved forward and in spite of very heavy Machine Gun fire from which the flat country gave absolutely no protection established to the N.E. SPRIETE and DESSELGHEM were taken and positions established in the hostile outskirts of "B" Company had taken up the position a strong party of the enemy advanced along the LEEMPUT – SPRIETE Road and attempted to counter-attack. They were caught by the fire of our Lewis guns and driven off with heavy casualties. Through the fire of our position "A" and "C" Companies pressed on to the attack of DRIES and SPRAATE "C" Company succeeded in taking SPRAATE in spite of most determined resistance establishing a line from C.13 Central to C.15.d.9.1 at 4.0 a.m. This objective being reached	

WAR DIARY or INTELLIGENCE SUMMARY

Army Form C. 2118.

Place	Date	Hour	Summary of Events and Information	Remarks and references to Appendices
			B Company Commander ready to push forward for met with strong Resistance at C.15.b.8.0. Captain E.W. McClelland being wounded in the first in immediate counter attack in face drove in our most advanced troops slightly, but C and D Companies again pushed forward and forced in hand many the enemy attacks of the village. The enemy was still holding position in the left flank MONTEDEM at C.14. a.9.7 and the river front. So the remainder in attack by D Company from SPROATE in conjunction with a party which advanced along the flank of the 6/3 achieved this position which was then occupied by us. Our troops however several machine guns and a number of prisoners were taken by us. At 08.00 a strong enemy attack S.E. occurred on the line of the left boundary was rendered and repulsed. A Company advanced towards DRIES with without resistance, was no down was boundary. Ring resulted the line C.2.1.8.9.5.6.22.a.15 was they came across the what extensive trenches from the line of had night which there was but it was soon discovered that these were unoccupied by a strong party	

WAR DIARY or INTELLIGENCE SUMMARY

Army Form C. 2118.

Sheet 5

Place	Date	Hour	Summary of Events and Information	Remarks and references to Appendices
	19th October		As "B" Company which was to join in the attack was being heavily shelled from their flanks and from enemy shelling the O.C. "A" Coy decided to withdraw his right flank and consolidate the line G.21.b.8.9. to G.21.b.7.0. At 12.30 the O.C. "A" Company received orders from the Commanding Officer to make another attempt to secure the village DRIES. Since this time he advanced round the north side of the village and cleared it up to G.15.c.2.2. but on passing this point the machine gun fire from the east houses and from G.16.c.4.5. was so intense that it was quite impossible to advance over the flat stretch of ground which had to be crossed to reach this portion of the O.C. "A" Company decided to hold this former line whilst he consolidated. On receiving this report of the situation the Commanding Officer however that the troops were going to advance were on front in a S.E. direction decided not to make any further attempt to take this position except in conjunction with them.	
	20th October		At 06.00 the 1st Battn. The Royal Innishkilling Fusiliers had moved into work pertaining the line G.15.a.5.5. – G.15.c.9.1. – G.22.d.7.5. thus having	

WAR DIARY or INTELLIGENCE SUMMARY

Army Form C. 2118.

Place	Date	Hour	Summary of Events and Information	Remarks and references to Appendices
Sheet 6.	20th October		completed when Turks had formed a very [strong?] line for the 102th Brigade to cover its canal and advance in a S.E direction. The 102th Brigade came up from the L.F's and advanced in a S.E direction. The Battalion still holding the line as protection for the flank. During the day it was ascertained that the enemy who were entering the L.F's in the N.E by O.H.E.M would advance and at 15.00 they were seen coming forward. This cleared the trees at 6.15 a.s.s to 6.10, 8.9.5 and "D" Company trenches with them at 6.9 to 7.30 at 16.00 at 12.00 orders were received that the 12th R. Irish Rifles would relieve the 1st Batt. The Royal Inniskilling Fusiliers who relieved little fire without incident and the 109th Brigade being now in support. The Battalion was billeted in O.25 a. Battalion Headquarters at 6.25 w 2.8. The whole Battalion being reported in billets by 16.00 on May 21st.	109th Bd. HS.
	21st October		During this most difficult operation the Battalion advanced a distance of 2,100 yards on a front that started at 1,200 yards and increased to 2,500 yards culminating in villages and about 60 prisoners and a large number of Machine Guns. The situation was rendered the more difficult by the fact that a very	

Sheet 7.

WAR DIARY
or
INTELLIGENCE SUMMARY.

Army Form C. 2118.

Place	Date	Hour	Summary of Events and Information	Remarks and references to Appendices
	21st Oct/14		Large track of country had to be covered in the dark by a comparatively small force and by the shortage of Officers. The casualties during this operation were Officers 3 wounded :— Capt. E.W. McLellan. Capt. I.A. Worsley. M.C. 2/Lieut. G. H. Bonner. (Connaught Rangers Attached) Other Ranks :— Killed 17. Wounded 42. Missing 14. Casualties inflicted on the enemy are unknown but however at our own ranks they left a lot of dead on the captured ground.	

Signed,
Commander ?, 2nd Bn Royal Inniskilling Fusiliers.

WAR DIARY or INTELLIGENCE SUMMARY

Army Form C. 2118.

Place	Date	Hour	Summary of Events and Information	Remarks and references to Appendices
	October 22nd		The Battalion and Companies are unengaged	
	23rd		The 109 Brigade moved forward into the line. The Battalion being in support in J.19.c and d. Battalion Head Quarters at I.19.d.9.1.	109th Bde. HLtr. HQrs. (Std Order 69)
	24th		Orders were received at 23.30 for a general attack to take place at 09.00 the following morning. This order was immediately communicated verbally to the Company Commanders by the Commanding Officer. B and C Companies being ordered to form the front line of the attack. A Company in support and D Company in reserve. B and C Companies had to take up their positions of attack in the open before dawn and they moved to the line J.26.a.9.0 to J.26.b.1.9. This movement being completed at 04.30.	
	25th		Shortly before Zero hour "A" Company moved forward and moved in the rear rear and at Zero advanced behind the other two Companies. D Company moved forward to J.19.d or Zero hour and Battalion Head quarters were established at J.20.c.0.0.	

Army Form C. 2118.

WAR DIARY
or
INTELLIGENCE SUMMARY.
(Erase heading not required.)

Instructions regarding War Diaries and Intelligence Summaries are contained in F. S. Regs., Part II. and the Staff Manual respectively. Title pages will be prepared in manuscript.

Place	Date	Hour	Summary of Events and Information	Remarks and references to Appendices
	25th		When our barrage lifted the 1m S26d4.1-J27a1.5 at 09.00 the leading companies moved up to it and followed it closely. When it moved forward at 09.03 As soon as the advance commenced heavy M.G. fire was opened from numerous M.G. posts hidden in hedges and near farms. These on our front were soon overtaken, and allowed, and at 09.40 the left Company Commander reported that he had reached the line J33d0.2 to J33d4.7 and was advancing. At 10.00 Battalion HeadQuarters moved forward to J26b8.9. As the advance continued the Battalion came under extremely heavy M.G. fire from the ridge on the left flank running through J26 and J34 which was strongly held by the enemy with numerous Machine Guns. It felt that the ridge had not been cleared and at 12.00 our front companies were to lose direction somewhat to the right and at 12.00 our front companies were on the line J32d52 to J33d38 in touch with the 9th Division on the right and with the 2nd Batt. Royal Inniskilling Fusiliers on the left.	

D. D. & L., London, E.C. (A8204) Wt. W2171/M231 759,000 5/17 Sch. 53 Forms/C2118/14

WAR DIARY or INTELLIGENCE SUMMARY

Army Form C. 2118.

Place	Date	Hour	Summary of Events and Information	Remarks and references to Appendices
	Oct 25th		and A Company in support at J33d O.q. At this point the intense MG fire from the B.M flank which was now enfiladed made a further advance in the original direction impossible though the leading companies tried to press forward towards BERGWIJK but Johnson and 2 Lieut Seracy being wounded it [was] little being able to remain at 3.30. At 14.00 the commanding Officer sent forward Blenkharn to J33d O.q. with orders to assume command for an attack towards KLEINBERG. This attack was however postponed and D Company remained at J33d O.q. At 16.30 orders were received from 103rd Brigade that this attack should be carried out under a barrage at 11.00 though. Runners were immediately despatched to the companies the orders only reached them about two minutes before zero. In spite of this the C and D Companies followed by A Company in support of their companies and went forward shortly after the barrage. B and C Companies at the conclusion advanced in the direction of KASKENSTRAAT. This advance was carried out under extremely heavy medium gun fire in spite of which	Vid SD57

WAR DIARY
or
INTELLIGENCE SUMMARY.
(Erase heading not required.)

Army Form C. 2118.

Place	Date	Hour	Summary of Events and Information	Remarks and references to Appendices
	Oct 25	9 P	A and D Companies gained the line of the road J34c29 to J34c28 being in touch with the 2nd Battalion Royal Inniskillings Fusiliers on the left. "B and C Company contracted the form D.b.c.2.6 when they came under very heavy enfilade fire from the KLEIN BERG ridge and being in all to maintain their positions retired to their former positions in J33d. At 22.10 orders were received from Brigade that the line which had been reached should be consolidated and the OC Commanding Officer made the following dispositions — B Company R P3659 A Company J34c29 C Company J33d65 "D" Company J34a25	109th Bde RJ 4.
	26		The positions were consolidated during the night. The day passed quietly at 14.30 patrols were sent out to keep touch with the enemy. They came under hostile machine gun fire immediately after leaving our lines so the enemy were still holding ULSTER HOEK KLEIN BERG RIDGE in strength being dug in along the road running through Stenbeek No overnight post was started and Companies [?] was arranged that it should be taken over by the 9th Division	

Army Form C. 2118.

WAR DIARY
or
INTELLIGENCE SUMMARY.
(Erase heading not required.)

Place	Date	Hour	Summary of Events and Information	Remarks and references to Appendices
	27th		and when darkness fell B company was relieved by the 9th Royal Scottish Rifles and was withdrawn to support at J.33.d.0.90. C company was ordered to hold the farm at J.33.d.6.5 with a post and to establish a liaison post at J.33.d.6.5 and withdrew the remainder of B in company to J.33.a.9.0.	
			Patrol was again sent out by us to keep touch with the enemy and at midnight 12.00 they were still to push forward up the hill and over when line was advanced under considerable MG fire to the line J.29.c.50.25 to J.34.b.6.10 to P.4.a.9.9. Orders were received from Brigade that our line should be established there and no further advance made in strength, though patrols should push forward. In enemy still held a line along the top of the ridge near road J.35.a.5.0 to P.29.q.5.5 In the evening the Battalion was relieved by the 2/4th Queens Royal West Surrey Regiment. and marched to HULSTE. They billeted in Bibustra (windries) during the night. 24th Somme wounded today. CRO Killed 5. Wounded his Messerret	Battn Order No 126. Battn Order No 124.
	28th 29th 30-31		The Battalion moved to HULSTE. The Battalion marched to ST ANNES. Rest and reorganisation and Presentation of gallantry ribbons after a month of many casualties falling. The strength of the Battalion on the 31st being 10 Officers, 256 other Ranks. Reviewed. Lieut Colonel Commdg. 1st Battn The Royal Inniskilling Fusiliers	

WAR DIARY
or
INTELLIGENCE SUMMARY.
(Erase heading not required.)

Army Form C. 2118.

1 R Innisk Fus
WO 3/4

Place	Date Nov	Hour	Summary of Events and Information	Remarks and references to Appendices
ST ANNE'S	1-10.		The Battalion was at ST ANNE'S. Training of Lewis Gunners, War Order drill, reorganization and Company training carried out daily under Company Commanders. On 9th the battalion is inspected in marching order by the Commanding Officer and on the 9th the GOC Xth Corps includes the 109th Brigade and distributes medals. 2Lt REF BRABAZON receives the MC and the following men received the MM. 200419 Sgt 49642 Pte Franklin. 49477 Sgt Longhurst. 19399 L/Cpl Clark. 3622 L/Cpl Heim. 42815 Pte Snater. 43986 Pte Thompson. 46009. Pte Blackwell. 18236 Sgt Thompson. 42041 Pte Waterhouse. 45043 Pte Groome. 47152 Pte Edwards. 13772 Pte Payne. The following were not present to receive their medals. 20074 Sgt /CSM Stewart. (Died of Wounds) 21238 Pte Summer. 28586 L/Cpl Shields 42977 A/Cpl McGovern 49554 Pte Jamill. 45777	✗ 42
	10-14		Company training under Company Commanders.	
RONCQ	15th		The Battalion moves to RONCQ. Marches at 10.00 and arrives at RONCQ at 14.00	Vide Batln Order 126.
	16th		Battalion parade presentation of Military Medals by the CO.	
	17th		Battalion attends Brigade Thanksgiving service	
	18th		Company training under Company Commanders. Received Tactical Exercises	

WAR DIARY
INTELLIGENCE SUMMARY

Army Form C. 2118.

Place	Date	Hour	Summary of Events and Information	Remarks and references to Appendices
	Nov 6th		The following decorations were awarded in the Battalion.	
			The Distinguished Service Order Lieut Colonel J R C Dewitt MC	
			Bar to the Military Cross Capt T W May MC	
			The Military Cross 2Lieut A F Roland. A/Captain J O N Hewitt A/Captain D N F Davidson A/Captain E W McClelland	
			The Distinguished Conduct Medal No 11713 Sergt G E Lowry. No 10875 Sergt R J Boyd. No 21572 Sergt C W Rea MM	
			No 44421 Lce Corpl J Palmer No 16701 Pte J A Dalrymple	
			Company Training. Brigade Tactical Exercises on 20th and 22nd	
	20-27th Nov		A guard of honour of 2Lieut G E Framingham MC and 2Lieut R F Roland MC and 50 Other Ranks is found from the Battalion to represent the 2nd Army at the Parade at TOURCOING when General Sir PLUMER GCB GCMG GCVO ADC. presents the flag of the 2nd Army to the city and receives a flag presented by the armies of the city. The parade takes place in front of the HOTEL DE VILLE at TOURCOING. The guard of the 1st Battn the Royal Inniskilling Fusiliers is first inspected by the general then the French Cavalry guard. The general then presents the flag and makes a short speech to which the Mayor replies and presents the flag of the city.	

WAR DIARY
or
INTELLIGENCE SUMMARY
(Erase heading not required.)

Army Form C. 2118.

Hour, Date, Place	Summary of Events and Information	Remarks and references to Appendices
November 23rd	The following decorations are awarded in the Battalion:—	
	The Distinguished Conduct Medal.	
	No 42112 Sgt A Wyer No 43054 LCpl R Brighton M549516 LCpl J Potter.	
	Company training. The Military Cross is awarded to 2Lieut J Kirwe.	
25th	The following officers join the Battalion:- 2Lt AA Heap, 2Lieut A Shunlock, 2Lieut D B Walker.	
26th	Brigade Tactical Exercise	
27th	Company training.	
28th	Brigade Tactical Exercise.	
29th + 30th	Company Training.	
	During the month of October attention was chiefly paid	
	to ammunition up drill Recreational Training, and Sport.	
	The Divisional League inter company matches were played off and	
	cross country runs were instituted.	
	The Strength of the Battalion on Nov 30th was 30 officers 1570 other Ranks.	

Bellew Lt Colonel.
Comdg. 1st Battn. The Royal Inniskilling Fusiliers.

WAR DIARY
or
INTELLIGENCE SUMMARY

Army Form C. 2118.

Hour, Date, Place	Summary of Events and Information	Remarks and references to Appendices
December RONCQ	The Ordinary routine for this month is:- 09:00 - 09:30 Company and B.H.Q. parades 09:30 - 12:00 Regimental Training / See order detail etc.	
3rd	Battalion Tactical Exercise.	
6th	Divisional Ceremonial Parade on Aerodrome at HALLUIN.	
7th	50 Officers 125 Other Ranks march to ROUBAIX to see His Majesty the KING pass through from TOURNAI to LILLE. The KING passes through RONCQ.	
8th		
9th	The following decorations awarded by the French Government. French Croix de Guerre à l'ordre Division (Silver Star) Lieut Colonel JRC DENT DSO MC Croix de Guerre à l'ordre Brigade (Bronze Star) Major A WALPOLE HOWARD. Capt DNF DAVIDSON MC Croix de Guerre à l'ordre Regiment. Capt J O'N HEWITT MC	

WAR DIARY
or
INTELLIGENCE SUMMARY
(Erase heading not required.)

Army Form C. 2118.

Instructions regarding War Diaries and Intelligence Summaries are contained in F. S. Regs., Part II. and the Staff Manual respectively. Title pages will be prepared in manuscript.

Hour, Date, Place	Summary of Events and Information	Remarks and references to Appendices
10th - 12th	Battalion practices for Divisional Ceremonial Parade.	
16th	Divisional Ceremonial Parade. The following message was received from Divisional Commander. "Congratulate all ranks of the Division on their smart turn out and soldierly bearing and marching at the Corps Commanders inspection today. The Corps Commander was extremely pleased with the appearance of the Divisions and with the whole parade."	
18th	Escort of 3 officers 100 O.Rs marches to TOURCOING Station to meet the colours party. Escort and colour marsch off from TOURCOING at 18. and arrive RONCQ 19.30.	
24th	His Majesty the King approves of the award of the VICTORIA CROSS to No 42954 Pte N HARVEY 1st Bn The Royal Inniskillin, Fusiliers	VICTORIA CROSS V.C. Recommendation.
26th	Battalion Parade at 09.00. The C.O. presents the ribbon of the VICTORIA CROSS to No 42954 Pte N HARVEY.	

WAR DIARY
or
INTELLIGENCE SUMMARY

(Erase heading not required.)

Army Form C. 2118.

Hour, Date, Place	Summary of Events and Information	Remarks and references to Appendices
31st	Battalion Cross Country run of 2½ miles instead of Brigade Field day. This month was chiefly devoted to sport of all descriptions. Boxing, running, football etc and to Educational Scheme. Demobilisation started by the husbanded men and miners going away.	

[signature] Lt Colonel.
Commdg 10th Battn The Royal Inniskilling Fusiliers.

Army Form C. 2118.

WAR DIARY
or
INTELLIGENCE SUMMARY

1ST BATTN.
THE ROYAL INNISKILLING FUSILIERS.

(Erase heading not required.)

Instructions regarding War Diaries and Intelligence Summaries are contained in F. S. Regs., Part II. and the Staff Manual respectively. Title pages will be prepared in manuscript.

V8/36

Hour, Date, Place	Summary of Events and Information	Remarks and references to Appendices
JANUARY 1919. RONCQ	The following awards were approved of by his Majesty the King:— Bar to DSO. Lieut Col J R C Dent DSO. MC. DCM 8389 Pte Mallock A Bln. 10757 Rft McKinney Aly. Belgian Authorities approved of the award of the CROIX de GUERRE to the following:— Capt C W B Fitzgerald. Connaught Rangers attd. 1st Royal Inniskilling Fusiliers. 9251 Sgt L Neary. C Coy. 18616 Sgt J Thompson. 9863. Sgt E Lauder. 27808. Pte W Doage MM. Brigade Ceremonial in Drill Hall. The colours are carried uncased. The Brigade forms a hollow square. 1st Battalion and the right of Battalion centre 2nd Battalion on the Left. The King's colour is uncased and presented to the 9th Battalion by Van de Isle CB. The Brigade move out of the hall and marches	

Army Form C. 2118.

WAR DIARY or INTELLIGENCE SUMMARY

1ST BATTN THE ROYAL INNISKILLING FUSILIERS

Volume 49

(Erase heading not required.)

Hour, Date, Place	Summary of Events and Information	Remarks and references to Appendices

RONCQ FEB 1919

3 — Capt E.N.V. Lawrence and 2Lieut R Shelley proceeded to England and struck off strength

4 — Major A.T.M. Gordon and 2Lieut R F Brabazon M.C. to England and struck off strength.

4 — Draft of 100 O.Ranks proceeded to join 1/6 Bn of same telling to and struck off strength.

11 — Major Air Howard and Capt N.P.L. boys to England and struck off strength.

14 — Capt D.N.F. Davidson M.C. + Lieut H.C. Stewart proceeded to England and struck off strength.

15 — The Corps Commander has awarded the Military Medal to N° 2076 Sergt J.A. Collins

WAR DIARY
or
INTELLIGENCE SUMMARY

(Erase heading not required.)

Volume 49

Army Form C. 2118.

Hour, Date, Place	Summary of Events and Information	Remarks and references to Appendices
24ᵗʰ	The Battalion won the XV Corps Cross Country Championship. In this race the Battalion represented the 6ᵗʰ (Welsh) Division. Medals were presented to the members of team and a silver cup to the individual winner No 49635 Pte Walch, 18ᵗʰ R. Inniskilling Fus.	
27ᵗʰ	The Battalion represented the XV Corps in the V Army Cross Country Championship, but failed to get placed.	
28ᵗʰ	Lieut H. Stopford, provided for duty with D.A.D.R.T. Colours and struck off Strength. The indentured officers are permitted to wear Badges of rank.	

Army Form C. 2118.

WAR DIARY
or
INTELLIGENCE SUMMARY
(Erase heading not required.)

Volume 49

Hour, Date, Place	Summary of Events and Information	Remarks and references to Appendices

28. 2/Lieut Pasking Officer authorization
2nd Lieut R.F. Roland N.C. 2/Lieut J. McLean
" J. Malone N/C " " " Grantham
" G. Hopkinson.

All 212 other ranks proceeded to
Concentration Camp during the month
for demobilization

J.C. Weud. Lieut Col
Comdg Depot R. Innskilling 2.

WAR DIARY
INTELLIGENCE SUMMARY

Army Form C. 2118.

Hour, Date, Place	Summary of Events and Information	Remarks and references to Appendices
24	host the General in Spain. The MSM awarded for services in the field to 9251 Sgt L Neary. During the month of January, 5 officers and 102 O.Rs. proceeded to Concentration Camp for demobilisation. The strength of the Battalion at the end of the month being 27 Officers. 506 Other Ranks. The Battalion school work was continued and the education of the whole Battalion commenced. Educational work was done for two hours per day on Mondays, Wednesdays and Thursdays. Football and running, boxing etc were continued. The Battalion team winning the 3rd Divisional Cross Country Run.	

Signed.
Lieut Colonel.
Commanding, 1st Battn. The Royal Inniskilling Fusiliers.

I.F.
1st April 1919.

The,
D.A.G's Office
3rd Echelon
G.H.Qrs B.E.Force.

Herewith Original War
Diary for the month
of March 1919.

J. Redent Lieut Colonel
Comdg 1st Bt. Inniskilling Fus.

WAR DIARY
INTELLIGENCE SUMMARY

Army Form C. 2118.

1/5Th THE ROYAL INNISKILLING FUSILIERS

Vol 50

Hour, Date, Place	Summary of Events and Information	Remarks and references to Appendices
RONCQ. MARCH 1919. 2nd	The Battalion moved to Mouscron. 2/Lieuts officers are permitted to wear the badges of rank. B/Lieutenants pending officers notification in Gazette. Lieut R.F. Roland M.C., Lieut H. & 2/Lt Lindow M.C., J.D Malone M.C., J Watson to Grantham.	
	3. Lieut Hopkinson proceeded to report to D.A.D.R.T. Calais as Embarkation Officer and Lieut. St. Stewart abroad.	
MOUSCRON	4. Lieut to Grantham. Lieut Walker and 27 Other ranks proceeded to join 1/5th Bn Royal Inniskilling Fusiliers and struck off strength. Lieut J.M Barnett having Bell's fever. Lieut J Clancey 5/6 Bn transf to London Authority to wear badges of rank of Lieut pending notification in Gazette.	
	5. Lieut J.M. Barnett to England and struck off strength	
	9. Draft of 5 Other ranks transferred to 7/8 struck off. Ernis killing Fusiliers	

Army Form C. 2118.

WAR DIARY
INTELLIGENCE SUMMARY

(Erase heading not required.) 1/2 BN R INNISKILLING FUSILIERS

Hour, Date, Place	Summary of Events and Information	Remarks and references to Appendices
MOOSCRON MARCH 15	2/Lieut T.D. McCarthy authorised to wear badges of rank of Lieutenant pending Officers' notification. The following officers transferred to the 2nd Bn R. Inniskilling Fus: Capt. C.W.B. Fitzgerald — Lieut J King M.C. Lieut J Busby M.C. — Capt to Major MC 2/Lieut D.N O'Toole M.M — 2/Lieut to T/P/G Lieut. Rev Adamson The following officers and Other Ranks transferred to the 9th Bn R. Inniskilling Fusiliers. Capt G Moore M.C. — Lieut F.P.H. Bull. Lieut J Busby M.C. — Lieut A.F. Foley. Lieut. E.A. Murphy. — Lieut A.L. Healy and 23 other Ranks. Draft of 9 other Ranks transferred to be 1/6 R.Battalion R Innis Fus. The Battalion headed by the Band of the 2nd Bn Royal Inniskilling Fusiliers marched	

1247 W 3299 200,000 (E) 8/14 J.B.C. & A. Forms/C-2118/11.

Army Form C. 2118.

WAR DIARY
or
INTELLIGENCE SUMMARY
(Erase heading not required.) 1ST BN THE ROYAL INNISKILLING FUSILIERS

Hour, Date, Place		Summary of Events and Information	Remarks and references to Appendices
DUNKERQUE	18	from Lille to Mouscron 5th and entrained for DUNKERQUE 15.30	
	26	Battalion arrived in DUNKERQUE 03.00 Embarked at DUNKERQUE for SOUTHAMPTON.	
	28	Arrived at SOUTHAMPTON 08.00 Entrained for TIDWORTH and marched to CANDAHAR BARRACKS. Transferred to 2nd Bn P. Innishkilling Fus during month 4 Off 108.	
		" " 1/6" " — — 2 Off 42 OR	
		" " 9th " — — 6 Off 23 OR	
		" " Sensitive " — — 62 O Ranks	
		Strength of Bn. 4 Off 46 Other Ranks.	
		Lt Col J.R.C. Dent D.S.O., M.C. Commanding.	
		Capt R.W.W. Stephenson. M.C. Adjutant	
		Capt G.E. Framingham M.C. Q.M.	
		Lieut R.F. Roland M.C.	
		[signatures]	
		Cmdg. 1 R. Inniskilling Fus	

www.ingramcontent.com/pod-product-compliance
Lightning Source LLC
Chambersburg PA
CBHW081543160426
43191CB00011B/1830